DIRTY TALK

A Simple Guide on How to Talk Dirty, Become More Confident, and Improve Your Sex Life Using Only Dirty Words

(Over 369 Examples of Dirty Talk Included–Guaranteed to Drive Him Wild!)

Mila Lebedev

Table of Contents

SPECIAL BONUS!

Get this additional Mastering the Art of Seduction Book 100% FREE!

Hundreds of others are already enjoying insider access to all of my current and future full-length books, 100% free!

If you want insider access plus this Mastering the Art of Seduction Book, all you have to do is **scan the code below** with your smartphone camera to claim your offer!

INTRODUCTION

Are you new to talking dirty and searching for ways to spice up your sex life? Do you seek to overcome your inhibitions in talking dirty? Do you want to learn a lot of dirty talk sayings and increase sexual pleasure? Do you desire to learn step-by-step the basics of talking dirty? Then I should congratulate you on purchasing this book because it contains the perfect information you need to empower yourself in the bedroom and own your man.

Many years ago, I was having a conversation with a friend of mine, and she was distraught. She complained of how she couldn't just seem to please her man in the bedroom anymore. She had recently gotten whips and handcuffs to try to make their sexual life more exciting, but nothing changed.

The first question I asked was," what type of conversations do you have in the bedroom?" but she didn't seem to understand. All they did was a bit of foreplay, and then the sex. It was mostly moaning and gasping, and there was no sort of conversation, no form of "Talking"; I termed it "Silent Sex."

Silent sex doesn't necessarily mean "soundless sex"; it refers to sex without communication. No underlying conversation to understand your partner's needs, no "Dirty Talk."

I realized this scenario my friend described to me was a prevailing situation among my close friends; great sex at the start of the relationship, and over time it becomes monotonous. What they had in common was that they didn't engage their partners in stimulating conversations in the bedroom. By conversation, I don't mean to talk about the milk running out or the clogged sink–Definitely not! In plain terms, I am referring to sensual, exciting, and good old dirty talk!

I, myself wasn't immune to these problems. I loved sex but was very shy, didn't want to talk about anything in bed, made the faintest sounds until it began to feel I was losing everything. I screamed for help, and it saved me and got me the man of my dream. My secret? Understanding the effect of talking dirty.

Nobody was born with the ability to know the right things to say during sex; it is a skill that is acquired and learned over time with dedication and practice, or from the experience of others, which is the case with this book.

By downloading this book, I believe congratulations are for actively taking the first step towards a new and more exciting sexual life. Towards understanding the secret language of desire that not only teaches how to increase sexual tension between you and your partner but also how to make him obsessed with you!

Is this book for me?

For some reading this book, maybe you don't have much of sexual life. Still, you intend to solidify your knowledge before taking the next step in your relationship, or perhaps you are hoping to find new ways of renewing your dying sex life, or maybe you are reading this book because you seek to overcome shyness and awkwardness in sexual activities or perhaps you are reading just for the fun of it! I guarantee there is a bit of something for everyone.

Possibly, you might have read a couple of self-help books on talking dirty, but all attempts to improve your sex life ended in tears. However, before burying yourself into this book, you need to make a promise, promise to be open-minded, begin the book on a clean slate, ready to take on every bit of information. This is the only way to benefit from this book.

This book contains information ranging from the psychology and benefits of dirty talk, how to get your man in the mood, how to overcome your fears and inhibitions, how to introduce the talk to yourself and your man, common mistakes to avoid, how to use skype and video calls in dirty talking, how to sext, secrets to role play, and lots more.

This book was written, taking into account lots of real-life scenarios and situations that I proffered long-lasting solutions to, and I expect it to be your daily guide to a great sexual life. There's a lot of space in the margin for you to make jottings and write down how you intend to apply every sentence that you read. Adding something as minute as a simple, well-executed dirty talk can drastically turn around your sexual life.

The skills you are about to acquire will make you not only a maestro in the bedroom but also a master in the art of verbal seduction.

Mila Lebedev

Chapter 1: The Psychology Behind Dirty Talk

Building Tension

A friend of mine, Rebecca, is a gentlewoman who loves sex a lot. But, now, she and her husband aren't feeling the passion anymore, and she knows he is slipping away, soon to be taken by a woman with a big ass, full breasts, and some mad sex skills. How can she save her marriage? I told her about dirty talking during sex, and her reply was, *"Nah, Michael is too good to want something that freaky."* And she felt shy. But, after a trial, she enjoyed mind-blowing sex. Michael was surprised, but he didn't stop her. This begets the question, what's the psychology behind dirty talking?

I know the reason you are here is that you are frustrated with being normal. You are tired of lying on your back or bending on a table or lying on all fours, and your man drives his dick into you for a couple of minutes, and you stay soundless, disabled with shyness. Hence, in this chapter, we will discuss the psychology behind the dirty talk, it's importance, how to get your man in the mood, the power of talking dirty in creating intimacy even when your man isn't close by, and finally, the secret and power of sexting which will make him crazy about you and spice up your sex life.

I never believed I would be a dirty talker until I tried it. I loved sex a lot but felt inferior, very shy. I never envisioned myself as someone who would say, *"Yes, baby, caress me; I am a bad girl."*... WTF! However, trying it for the first time sent waves and waves of orgasms into my sex life. It made me love sex more, and I always anticipate every sexual opportunity. Why does dirty talking turn people on? Let's find out.

A good reason why people dirty talk during sex is because sex is a stress relief which makes people less aware of the words they say or the actions they take during it. Studies have shown that when you have an orgasm, Oxytocin, which is a chemical that reduces stress, is released from your body. When this stress is being released, it prompts you to say your sexual wants and feelings, things you wouldn't say on a typical day. I remember a time when I was having sex, and I said, *"I've been a very naughty girl, Baby. Fuck me, Hard!"* It was what I wanted that moment, and it sent me to the heavens. Usually, would I have said that? Definitely **NOT**. I'm a grown-up woman, but it felt good to be a naughty girl, and I had an orgasmic reward. Most times, you may want to say something dirty about your man's body or yours, but you wouldn't say it because of ethics. Later, you find yourself saying it freely during sex. Don't be turned off or shocked; you want it!

Did you know that your brain determines the success and failure of every dirty talk? I bet you didn't! Trust me; it isn't all about the sex organ. Although they have their importance and personally, a good dick will always beat the best vibrator. However, brain importance remains unmatched. Its role in achieving sexual pleasure is enormous, and it stands at the gateway between you being in the mood or not in the mood. This is why you would most likely not enjoy sex when tired, stressed, or sad. Dirty talk switches on the part of your brain responsible for sexual pleasure, and once you aren't tired or anxious, you begin to get into the mood.

Dirty talking arouses the amygdala, a part of our brain that regulates fear, excitement, and sexual pleasure. This means that you can get sexual pleasure by becoming the dirty talker and keeping your partner in constant anticipation of what you plan to do to them. Let me paint you a scenario: imagine you are in a cowgirl position, and your man's hands are on your ass. Then, you straddled his dick and asked, *"How do you want me to fuck you? Like this?"* and you begin to ride him slowly, then fast and back to slow motion. If you enjoy that, then you are dominant, which is good, and you are keeping the element of surprise, which makes the sex more exciting. But, if you don't want to be dominant, there is no harm in being dominated and becoming his submissive telling him to drill you hard.

Generally, dirty talk can improve your sex life and shouldn't be limited to the bedroom. Studies have shown that using dirty talks during the day has a lot of effects on sexual pleasure between partners. It doesn't need to be loud or complicated; just keep it simple yet spicy. There was one time I visited my boyfriend in his workplace, and while he was talking on the phone, I whispered into his ears, *"Do you think I have panties on right now? Too bad, you can't find out."* Then I left him immediately and went home. After work, he barged into the room, almost tearing his clothes, and I knew *Fuckmenia* has begun. If you don't enjoy dirty talk outside the bedroom, it's okay because I know you might be afraid of people overhearing your conversation. However, dirty talking outside the bedroom will surely add spice and build sexual tensions in public places...

Nevertheless, it's okay if you don't want to talk dirty. However, if you find it hot and sexy, I urge you to give it a try. Surprise your man, get a grip over him, *girl*. Make him look forward to the sex; make him think about fucking you before doing it. It makes the pleasure worth it. That's the definition of sexy!

Now I know you must wonder, *"What's the hype all about?"* Why is dirty talking important in spicing up my sex life? I should tell you; the answer is simple!

With dirty talking, you will be able to create sexual tension. Sexual tension is vital in spicing up the sex and making it enjoyable. Sadly, most women don't take note of their lover's desire, which is a significant reason why sexual relationships gradually deteriorate. Creating sexual tension leaves an image of you in the brain of your lover. Your words supported with your sexy actions are all it takes to create the sexual tension required to arouse your lover, who typically shows a lack of interest in sexual activities. Put on a good pair of heels, wear a dress that will leave a lasting impression on him and pay him a visit in his workplace, tell him how much you want to fuck him, and ride his face and fake sadness because it's not possible because of his job. I bet you after you leave, the song *Wild thoughts by Rihanna* will be playing in his head, and he will be sexually tensed with wild ideas of you. Every minute and hour till he get home will be flooded with naughty thoughts of you. He will be fucking you in his mind.

On the other hand, don't make him sexually tensed and leave him, it's dangerous, and you may lose him due to frustration. But, use it to make him aroused. If your man is on an assignment in another city or he is cut up in some things and very occupied. Do you know the amount of sexual tension you will cause if you say, *"I miss you, baby, when will I see you?"* I bet you would see him sooner than expected.

Now, after the sexual tension has been scored and both of you are in heat, like hungry lions looking at prey, you devour each other intensely. Your sex becomes intensifying. Now during sex, the dirty talk also defines the intensity. You would know if you need to talk calmly or scream crazily. The goal is to drive him crazy! Make him fuck you physically and mentally. When you whisper words like, *"Yeah, baby, this is lovely, I want all of you,"* into his ear, he flows with it, and you would be surprised that soon he will be following your command, giving it to you harder when you scream, *"harder." You* will even intensify the present sex and future ones. Intensify the sex by talking about his actions and what you would love him to do to you. There is no harm in telling him you want him to cum on your boobs, and it only makes it more intensifying!

Finally, another reason why dirty talk is important is its effect on leaving an image of you, a sexy one, burning in the mind of your lover. You will be his first thought when he wakes up in the morning and the last when he goes to bed. I know it is lovely for your husband to think affectionately about you at all times. However, I should tell you that nothing keeps a man better than an obsession. If he becomes obsessed with what he does and what he is capable of doing to you, you will be on his mind *every time!*

Dirty talking ensures that he never forgets and keeps your fantasies in his mind. It doesn't matter if he is close by or not. With dirty talking, you own the bed, and no other woman can take your place.

Creating the mood

Dirty talk without mood and intimacy is a RED FLAG!
Chances of failure = 99%

The ladder to a successful dirty talk starts with mood and intimacy. If your partner isn't used to it, and you are a beginner, creating the mood works best. But most women are faced with the problem of building it. Let me teach you something simple. When I started to talk dirty, there was one method that always worked with my lover, and I have given it as advice to numerous women and yes! It has worked! **THE POWER OF DATE NIGHTS!**

I know date nights are used to get to know each other and eat good food. *However, have you imagined the effect it will have on your lover if you are the three-course meal on the menu?* It's a lot sexier and will spice up your sex life. It's easy to turn up the mood on a date night and enjoy brain-touching, skin-tingling, hot sex afterward, and it all gets down to your preparation.

Without a doubt, if you aren't in the mood for freakiness, then your partner isn't either. So, before you go on a date to meet up in the restaurant, you can decorate your bedroom (for starters). Use dim lights and keep every sex toy at close reach. You know that's the goal, mind-blowing sex. So, prepare that area. After that, work on your body, use lingerie that's sexy because he gets to see it later, which will drive him crazy, also apply moderate perfume. The ultimate goal is for him to see you as a prize he hasn't won. Then, dress up and get your man.

It's easy to get a man into the mood. If you understand the tricks of sexting, then I should congratulate you. If you don't, *don't worry,* I will give them to you in a nutshell. With sexting, you can get him in the mood before he sees you on the date. There is an easy trick I use to put my man in the mood, and you can do it too. I send him a picture of my thong before wearing it. Admittedly, I know he wants to see more, but I won't give him the pleasure. I need him to desire and want me, or if I want to be borderline naughty, I send him a picture with my hands covering my boobs. Sometimes, I use words instead of pictures. When we are already seated in the restaurant, I say, *"don't you want to touch, baby? I'm wet."* This always works, and most times, we end up not eating because I've got him thinking about me so much that he cannot handle it anymore.

When you want to create a mood, you just need to create the desire and want. There are numerous ways to do this and don't limit yourself to my ideas. Note that flirting can also put your man in the mood. But, learn to try new ideas because an idea when overused kills the desire.

Whenever I'm asked, *"why is creating the mood important?"* I always reply with another question. *"Why is foreplay important before sex?"* It's for the better sexual experience; the better the mood, the spicier the sex.

Dirty talk and a long-distance relationship

So, I've had my share of long-distance relationships, and it constitutes a significant part of my breakups because my exes ended up with other women, they cheated. Then, my anthem was *Men are scum*, and this went on for a while until a realization dawned on me. I realized that it wasn't that I lost those men because I wasn't beautiful or smart. But because I had no grip on them: sexually, emotionally, and intimately. Then, I discovered dirty talking, but it was too late. However, I believe this isn't your case, and there is still time to get that love back with some easy secrets of dirty talking using sexts.

When there is a lot of distance between you and your lover, dirty talking and sexting can come in handy. It helps you retain the intimacy and desire even when you aren't together. I know some people see sexting with the aid of pictures and videos as a step over the line. But, if you are one of those, I don't think you would be here trying to learn the art of dirty talking in a bid to save your man. To succeed in creating the desire, you need to be in the mood. It mustn't be forced; Let it flow. It's two's thing and should be enjoyed by both parties, not just as a means to save your boyfriend or lover. This is only when it will be useful. I know saying stuff like, *"I miss the feeling of you inside me, when are you coming back?"* May feel hard and awkward in the beginning, but I tell you it leaves an image of you in his mind. It makes you horny just like it makes him horny, and your intimacy becomes solid because you are buried in his thoughts.

I believe you might think that dirty talk and sexting can't save a long-distance relationship and make his day all about you. But, let me prove you wrong. Imagine you have a dog, and instead of feeding the dog a bone, you show him the bone and place it beyond his reach. It's not farfetched that the dog will do everything possible to get to the bone because he wants it; likewise, humans. When you dirty talk and sext, all he would want to do is see you, the desire in him will almost make him devour you when you meet in due time. Now, let's move to a topic you have been waiting for...

Sexting

From the beginning of this chapter, I have stressed the word *"sexting"* a couple of times because it is a part of dirty talk that can't be neglected.

First, I should emphatically state that sexting isn't harmful; it is healthy, and your shyness shouldn't be a hindrance from enjoying its benefits. Surely there's a possibility that you might have heard news and rumors about sexting with pictures that went wrong. However, I know your privacy is important, and I wouldn't want to tarnish it. This is why I'm going to give you secrets on how to successfully sext with pictures. But, before that, how do you build sexual tension with sexting?

Most times, I do call myself the head of shy people association. But, surprisingly, the fact that I was shy didn't stop me from enjoying the numerous benefits of sexting. Do you want to know my little secret? Here we go!

Reminiscing

If you are stumped, maybe because you are shy, then an excellent way to sext is to begin from experiences. Let your man know what he has sexually done that you loved, and it's always right to hype these experiences. You could say, *"Babe, do you remember that one time we were in the bedroom and we had sex with my panties on? It was awesome. Can we try it next time?"* Great! He is smiling somewhere, thinking about it. Soon, he will be sharing his own experiences, and you guys are both turned on and smiling at the same time. It is the easiest way to get started because most guys won't get turned on quickly when you begin sexting by saying, *"Baby, let me see you,"* or *"I want you."* If you have tried it by using this kind of statement and it was unsuccessful; it doesn't mean that you are wrong, but you just used the statement at the wrong time. After you have made him remember those times like a champ, then we move to the next step.

Prompting

After opening hidden memories, then comes the encouragement and prompting. Let me inform you that the success and duration of sexting is the encouragement poured into it. You need to persuade and encourage him. How do you do this? It's so simple. For instance, when I introduced my man to sexting, he wasn't convinced to send his dick pic to me. He saw his meat as ugly and not photogenic. But I encouraged him. Sometimes, when we sext, I say, *"all I want is to suck you hard and feel you inside me. Can I see your meat?"* Sometimes, he might want to give excuses like, *"I don't know. I've not had my bath; it's not fully hard."* But I always anticipated that, and I follow up immediately by saying, *"I want to see it!"* When he sends it, I reply, *"yummy!"* This makes him more relaxed and activates his freaky side. Encouragement cannot be neglected. Don't feel like he wants it more than you or you are doing your best. Encourage him sexily.

Teasing

Say this in your mind, **"teasing is important."** because yes, it is. You don't have to rush things; use the element of suspense. You kill the length and reduce the desire if you send your boobs or pussy picture at the beginning of the show. Don't do that, *girl.* Kill him with excitement. Why should you send him a picture of your vagina when you can send a picture of your panties? Make him want to see more, but share less. Tease him, baby. If you are shy about showing those assets, check the internet for some sexy couple's videos, send it to him, and add the tag, "you and me". It also does the trick.

Foreshadowing

After you have talked about past experiences, encouraged your man, teased him, then it's time to talk about the future. Most times, when you sext, your man isn't close by, and that moment all he wants is just to see you. But, he can't, right? So, how do we preserve those desires and ensure that when you meet your lover, it's going to be sexually intense, just like the days of sexting? It's easy. When I sext, I usually end with some sexts like, *"I want to fuck in the shower. I love the cold feeling of water and the hard throbbing of your cock in me at the same time. Can we do that next time?"* Surely, it's going to be a *"yes,"* and both of us will be looking forward to it. Make him think about the future happening, that's why foreshadowing is essential. But those are the words I love, and you can stick to the simple, *"can we try it tomorrow? I've got new lingerie." These words usually set the tone for an exhilarating sexual encounter with your partner.*

Yeah, there you have it, the four secrets to sexting. I will be disappointed if you just read this and don't apply it. Please, don't disappoint me.

So, I promise to teach you secrets/precautions for your pictures during sexting to prevent them from going viral, and I'm not one to break my promise. But I will also teach you how to sext with emoji's because, let's admit it, not everyone loves to text. So, here are the secrets to safe picture sexting.

- Don't be forced to send your pictures. It's something that must be done voluntarily, and if you don't want to do it, then DON'T. Stick to words if you are uncomfortable with pictures. Don't be forced!

- Trust. I know it's easy to believe the *"It's for my eyes only"* trick, and most women have fallen for this. We both don't want to see your pictures on porn hub or X-videos, or even worse, social media platforms like Twitter, WhatsApp, and Facebook. So, if you don't trust your man, then don't send your pictures, and even when you trust him, reiterate the fact that it's solely for him.

- Vagueness is important. You know, your man only wants to see your boobs, ass, and other stuff when sexting. So, why include your face? Be a smart girl. Even if your man is trustworthy, there are hackers everywhere, and mistakes do happen. So, make sure your nudes can't be linked to you. Do you have a tattoo known by everyone? Don't put it in the picture.

This makes you less scared of your nudes leaking, and you can sleep with no worries.

- Assumed pictures are cool. You know sending someone your full boobs picture takes a truckload of trust. So instead of giving him the whole package, you can provide him with something close to that but with the same effect. Sending a side view of your boobs or a picture of your hands covering part of your boobs has the same effect as submitting the whole deal. You can send a picture of your body in a wet towel. OMG! It has more impact than your real boobs or ass.

- Delete, delete, delete if you aren't comfortable, and immediately remove after he sees them. Whenever I use WhatsApp, and I don't feel safe, I use the *delete for everyone's* option immediately.

Now I have given you the secrets, and I believe you would use them whenever you want to send him that picture because I'm going to be hurt if you do not use them.

Finally, how do you sext with emoji's?

Okay, you might need a mobile dictionary to fully use this because it's a big turnoff if a guy sends you 🧦, and you ask, *"Do you want an eggplant, baby?"* Be fast, babe! That's not what he means! Here are a list of emoji's and their sexual meaning.

- 🍆 =Dick

- 🍑 =Ass, Butt.

- 👌 =Pussy or Anal.

  These are the majorly used emoji's. Now, let's check out some phrases:

- 💦 THIS means I'm wet.

- 🍆 🍩 Can mean, let's fuck, or I want some mind-blowing anal sex.

- 👅 🍑 💦 Means I'm going to lick you till you cum.

- 💨 🍆 😲 Means I'm going to suck you, and it's going to blow your mind.

Most emoji's related to sex are food emoji's. However, the lists of useful emoji's for dirty talking aren't limited to the ones provided here. Now I believed you have learned something new and are planning to give it to him hot tonight. Please do, I'm sure you won't be disappointed.

FACT: Did you know that using emoji's while texting or rather sexting with that potential sex partner or even a lover who seems distant is one sure way to rekindle your sex life and ensure that your relationship remains raunchy and exciting? An online survey on 275 couples showed that 83 percent of those who used emoji's in their sext, regardless of the type of sexy emoji, tend to enjoy fantastic sex and make the experience outside sex worthwhile. So, if you aren't sexting with emoji's, you are probably missing the secret recipe to building sexual tension, encouraging intimacy even when your lover is distant, and limiting yourself from fantastic sex life.

SUMMARY

The psychology behind dirty talking

- ✓ It is a stress relief
- ✓ It arouses the brain, which makes the sex more pleasurable
- ✓ It improves sex life.

Why is it important?

- ✓ It increases sexual tension, makes sex intensify, and leaves an image of you in his daily thoughts.

Creating the mood

- ✓ The ladder to a successful dirty talking starts with mood and intimacy.
- ✓ Don't underestimate date nights.
- ✓ Create the desire, and you have the mood.

Dirty talk and a long-distance relationship

- ✓ Don't force it; let it flow. Enjoying it is the goal.
- ✓ Use sexting and dirty talking to make him always think of you.

Sexting

- ✓ It's the key to preserving your relationship.

The four secrets of sexting

- ✓ Reminiscing: talk of the past.
- ✓ Prompting: encourage him.
- ✓ Teasing: the more he wants to see, the less you reveal
- ✓ Foreshadowing: make him think of future Sexcapades.

Chapter 2: Preparing for The Dirty Talk

Tackling inhibitions & building confidence

I met some women in 2015, and they needed advice on ways to spice up their sex life. It didn't come as a surprise because if a woman likes someone, she would do anything and go to any length to keep that person. Back to my story... So, I advised them to talk dirty, *be the woman your lover always dreamt about*. But that idea was turned down almost immediately. Surprisingly, some of these women were talkers, but they just couldn't; they could stand before a thousand eyes and speak for hours. But they were shy and couldn't say to their man, *"You know I love it when you stick it up in my ass."*

Although most of these women left with other solutions, I still wondered why they were shy since it's someone intimate with them.

So, I want to ask you a question, and I want you to be honest with me. Are you shy about dirty talks? Think about that for some seconds. If you aren't, I'm happy for you. But if you are indeed shy, I promise you that you won't be shy after reading this chapter and following its instructions because it covers a practical approach on how to overcome shyness, how to overcome inhibitions, the importance of confidence, why you may be lacking it, and how to build your confidence. So, sit tight and open your brain to this sweet information.

My childhood was filled with shyness and low self-esteem, and this affected my sex life. I was the perfect synonym of the word "shy," and my boyfriend knew. Whenever we wanted to have sex, I always make sure the lights were off and would never dirty talk. I knew some people find it romantic to look into their lover's eyes when fucking, saying some things I termed "nasty" at that time. But for me, it was a straight No! I think you should know the consequences of my shyness because my greatest fear began knocking on the door. My boyfriend, although I saw him daily, seemed distant. Then, I knew I needed to act fast. After seeking numerous help, attending seminars, and reading various useful and useless pieces of stuff online, I finally found a secret, and I overcame my shyness and opened the doors of dirty talking. I want to share that secret because I believe it will help you get a better grip on your man.

How to overcome shyness in dirty talk

Overcoming shyness in dirty talks is quite easy, and you don't have to be scared of being called "nasty" or "slutty," if you follow these simple instructions.

First, **it doesn't have to be +18.** Yes, I know you are in search of your sexual calling and would kill to be your man's, Mia Khalifa. However, it is best to start slowly. Your goal isn't to say the nastiest word but to have the sexiest effect on your man. You might have seen some porn video where the woman said some ugly things, and it drives the man crazy, which will make you want to try it. But, my advice, **don't learn dirty talking from porn videos;** leave dirty talks in porn videos for porn stars because it will most likely not work for your man. Saying statements like, *"I want you, so bad."* is useful if you are comfortable with it. No law states you must start with comments like, *"I want you to bury your dick into my cunt and make me yours!"* Keep it simple.

Another way to rid yourself of shyness is to **dirty talk like an instructor.** (Spoiler alert: this was my first step into overcoming shyness.) If you are shy and don't know what to say, you can start by giving instructions. Sometimes when I'm with my man, and he is showing me his cunnilingus skills, I say, *"Ooh, just like that baby, yeah, you are going to make me cum."* I'm instructing him on the way I liked to be licked and also dirty talking. Get comfortable with him, tell him what you want him to do, guide him during foreplay, and you will begin to see that shyness fly out the window.

Watch the voice. The effect of every dirty talk is determined by the way you say the words. Sometimes, you don't need to talk aloud. Imagine you are in an event with your man, and you whisper into his ears, *"Baby - I'm wet."* Sexy, right? That's the power of the voice. You might have heard or seen videos where ladies scream dirty talks, don't follow it. If you are shy, say it softly with a sexy voice, and when everything gets intense, you wouldn't know when you would start to scream, *"Oh, fuck me."*

Practice when fully clothed. Most shy women always face the problem of combining nakedness and dirty talk. If you are one of these women, then it's safe to start practicing it while fully clothed. Send him a text on what you plan to do to him when he gets home, call him and tell him how you miss his cock, leave him a note telling him, *"too bad, you left for work without some juice."* When you do this over time, you become more comfortable. You won't be shy to say, *"I want you; can you stick it in?"* when you are with him.

Finally, another way to overcome shyness is to **seek help from a friend—liquor.** Usually, this would have been my first secret. But, it's always good to overcome shyness without liquor. However, if other methods seem hard, try this. Some shots of vodka, tequila, or beer loosen you up, and you will find yourself talking freely. Remember, I said *some* shots, so don't get drunk. You need the liquor to loosen up and not to lose control of yourself. Don't take it if it's going to make you feel bad. **Don't!** The goal is to spice it up, not to leave you thinking about the event of last night.

That's how I overcame my shyness and became a badass dirty talker. Are you having doubts? Don't. Because I tell you, there's no harm in trying. Funny enough, you might try and discover that you aren't timid and dirty talks aren't awkward, which opens the door to another level of sexual pleasure.

Sexual inhibitions and how to overcome them

Sexual inhibition is a booby trap for sexual behaviors, and they are common in everybody. Perhaps you have never heard of sexual inhibitions, but I'm sure somewhere, somehow, you have heard about sexual hang-ups (it means the same thing). Sexual inhibitions make people insecure and worried, which leads to a decline in sexual pleasure. I know as you read this, a particular inhibition will invade your mind but at the end of this chapter, be rest assured that it would be no more because you would have learned the secrets to overcoming common sexual inhibitions. Let's have an overlook on normal sexual inhibitions, shall we?

I am not immune to inhibitions, and I've had my share of them. There was a time when I couldn't walk naked in the house when my man is around because I felt I wasn't pretty, and I lacked the Amazonian body shape. I always put on my clothes after sex, and I ensured that the light stayed off even if my man protested. Then, I realized I had body shame and low self - esteem. Let me tell you a secret. That period, the sex wasn't good. I tried to avoid sexual pleasure as fast as possible. I know I'm not alone, and you might have experienced that too, especially if you have asked your man what's his type of woman. Instead of his reply to be "You," he starts to describe a woman with an hourglass shape like Nicki Minaj, and you know your boobs and ass aren't that much, which makes you embarrassed, and you begin to feel uncomfortable showing him your body. Moreover, according to an online survey on men and women, it revealed that over 60% of men admire their bodies more than women. So, it's perfectly normal to be scared of your body image as a lady.

You might be scared of your sexual experiences, which may be because you have been forced to have sex in your past relationships, and it's now affecting your present relationship. You might be scared that you won't be able to please the man of your dreams, scared that you won't have the same effect that female porn stars have on their men. Trust me, it's normal.

There was a time when I was in constant fear of sexual fantasies and sexual kinks. Although it is perfectly normal for a man to want some kinky sexual experience, I was scared and protective of my bodily health and self-esteem. That time, I have heard cases of women who were frightened of being bound or blindfolded because they had read news of women who tried it and got something else instead of mind-blowing sex with their partner. So, don't blame me for being scared. If you are afraid of BDSM or Voyeurism, even though it can add sparks to your sexual experiences, especially if your man wants it, it is understandable if you are afraid of it. I've been there. I remember one time when I was talking to a woman whose man wanted a threesome with two women. At first, she liked the idea, but when her friend was suggested as the third party, her fears kicked in, and she realized that she might lose her man, which made her refuse to go on with the plan. Of course, it affected her relationship, and she asked for my help in overcoming her inhibitions, which I assisted her, and she surmounted her fears. Now, it's your turn.

How then do you overcome inhibitions?

It is simple. Let's look at overcoming body image and low self-esteem. The only requirement to overcome this inhibition is to love yourself and love your body. I know you might be saying, "I love myself." Yes, that's true. But you need to tell yourself more. You are a masterpiece. If he says he fancies a big-breast lady and yours are small, show them proudly. Let him know that you are better than other ladies. Let me repeat it; LOVE YOUR BODY! Because it is the only way for good self-esteem and body image.

Also, learn to talk to your partner. Talk about sex, just like you would speak of his friends and your friends. Tell him your likes and dislikes, his fantasies that you can try, and those that are way over the line. Talk! When you keep quiet about it, it affects your sexual life and leads to other relationship problems. So, talk about your sexual fantasy inhibitions, talk about kinky sex. If you would love to try out BDSM with him, *tell!* If you find it disgusting, *talk!* If you don't know how to give him premium pleasure, *talk!*

This reduces stress and finally kills the inhibitions. It makes your man understand you, and you don't have to face it alone. Normally, talking isn't easy, especially if you are shy. However, the only solution to overcome shyness to talk is starting to talk. When you do this, after some seconds, you will see that you are comfortable and able to tackle your inhibitions adequately.

I was able to defeat my inhibitions when I began to trust my partner's actions when I started to see what has always been there. That is, he has my best interests in mind and wouldn't do anything to break me. So, if you are scared of sexual fantasies and kinky sex, you just need to trust your man. I know you might have had a terrible sexual experience and do not want to believe anything with a dick between the legs. But you have got to because not all men are scum! Trust him, and if you can't do that, then there is a problem, and you need to check yourself and your man to confirm your stand in the relationship. Your partner is meant to be trusted, not feared. Once you trust him, fulfilling your BDSM fantasy becomes easy because you know he can't hurt you, and he would stop when you say so. You know he can't fulfill his sex video fantasy with you and upload it on the internet or show it to his friends. Your partner should be trusted, so if you don't trust him, then you shouldn't be with him.

Finally, some women are terrified of their sexual performance, and this has caused bad sexual experiences and also become an inhibition. But, most of them don't know that overcoming this is very easy. Let's learn something from the men. You know when your man is fucking you, if you have taken note of this, he always watches for your reaction, your response to his strokes, and most men would dick you in a particular way for a while and ask, *"just like that?"* your answer would determine if he would maintain the pace, go deeper, faster, or slower. Likewise, you can also use that method. When on a doggy or cowgirl position with him, wiggle those butts on his dick and watch for his reaction. Watch out for his moans; then, you would know if to shake faster, slower, or switch to a killer blowjob.

I believe I have done an excellent job on this one for you. Now, we move to the last but equally important part of this chapter.

Building self- confidence

Michelle is a good friend of mine, and she came to me seeking answers to her problem. She loves dirty talk and finds it sexy, but whenever she tries it, it cracks her up and turns her off. Then she asked, *"How can I build my confidence in dirty talks?"* Hence, I'm going to use her case to answer your confidence problems.

Confidence in the dirty talk is crucial, even more, important than the words coming out of your mouth. Imagine you are in a missionary position with your lover, and you cover your face partially with your hands and speak inaudibly, *"fuck me harder."* Would he do it? I doubt that. Because it would be evident to him that you don't know what you want, and it will bring confusion and lead to a soft dick instead of a hard-on, or you say it audibly. Still, your facial expression shows that you are trying hard to remember some lines which he will interpret as *"you don't know what you want,"* and it will make him turned off and kill the sexual pleasure.

Trust me, I understand that dirty talking at the beginning needs a whole lot of courage and confidence because your man would notice the changes, and you don't want to feel embarrassed, shy, or look like a slut. Also, you might be scared of getting it all wrong and maybe confused about the right dirty word to use when he is on the boobs, eating you out, or fucking, and it kills your confidence, which makes you decide to moan than talk. However, finding your confidence is essential and a must for you if you want to dirty talk successfully.

How do you build this confidence?
The first step is to be comfortable. You need to get comfortable with the dirty talk. Do you think you would

be able to confidently say, *"I want your cum on my ass."* If you aren't comfortable with the word *"cum"*? You will sound awkward; Hence, the importance of being satisfied. The words flow better when you are comfortable with them. So, if *"I need your dick in me"* is too much for you, use *"I want you"* if it's convenient, and you can say it confidently with your hardened nipples.

Once comfortable, start the dirty talk slowly, let the tension build up before you activate the porn star mode. Starting with *"I'm your slut, make me yours."* can be on the high side, and it would most likely make your lover funnily look at you, which will kill your confidence. So, begin at the alphabet A with something like, *"I like it when you kiss my neck,"* or *"you look ravishing,"* and let it flow up.

You can build your confidence by telling your man how much sexual pleasure you are enjoying on the ride. Saying, *"oh, don't stop,"* isn't hard, and you won't look awkward. It is also a sexy compliment that puts more energy in your man's bones.

Finally, the last way to build confidence is to fake confidence. Suppress the urge to laugh at your words, put your passion into it. Look into his eyes as much as possible, be active and you will see your confidence grow. Very soon, you will be pouring out those sexy words without blinking your eyes, and your confidence will improve like that of a dirty talk goddess. **Remember, fake it till you can say it!**

Kristi and Gregory have been married for five years, and things are beginning to fall apart. He was a playboy when she met him, and she rocked his world, at least for four years and 11 months before everything came down. Gregory's excuse was she lacked the desire he enjoyed for the last few years, and Kristi felt her husband wasn't understanding. When they fell to the rock bottom, and we're almost on the verge of break up, they knew they had to see a counselor for their kids. Do you know what the counselor told them? "TALK," she said. Apparently, they talked to themselves instead of talking to each other. They began to speak...after a couple of hours; they both realized that the reason why Gregory feels Kristi lacked the desire he wants is that she was nurturing some inhibition, the fear of vulnerability. He wanted some sexual actions where she would be in vulnerable positions. Now talking about the inhibition rekindled the long-lost truth and even allowed the fulfillment of their various fantasies, and of course, their marriage blossomed. Be like Kristi and Gregory.

SUMMARY

How to overcome shyness in dirty talk

- ✓ It Doesn't Have to Be +18
- ✓ Don't Learn Dirty Talk from Porn Videos
- ✓ Dirty Talk Like an Instructor
- ✓ Watch the Voice
- ✓ Practice When Fully Clothed
- ✓ Seek Help from A Friend—Liquor

How to overcome inhibitions

- ✓ Love Your Body
- ✓ Learn to Speak with Your Partner
- ✓ Trust Your Partner
- ✓ Watch Out for His Reactions

How to build self-confidence

- ✓ Be Comfortable
- ✓ Dirty Talk Slowly
- ✓ Let Him Know You Are Enjoying It
- ✓ Fake It till You Can Say It

Chapter 3: Introducing the Talk

To Yourself

When I decided to try dirty talking, on the first night, I almost killed my dying sexual relationship with my boyfriend. I talked dirty to him, it started well, and then everything started to crumble. I said some words that turned him off instead of the other way around, and I cried afterward because we had to stop the sex. I began to wonder where I got it all wrong. Hence, I buried myself into more research and talked to some people, and then it dawned on me that I've not introduced the talk to myself. I realized that the knowledge I've learned, the confidence built, the shyness I surmounted were just brothers to dirty talking and not the talk itself. Without delay, I introduced it to myself and revived my almost dead sexual relationship, and I'm going to share how I did it with you.

To this end, this chapter will cover how to ease yourself into dirty talking, the Do's and Don'ts of dirty talking, how to get yourself comfortable, and finding that seductive voice that will blow your man's mind.

While searching for ways to introduce the dirty talk to myself, I met with a woman who asked me, *"Have you eased yourself into dirty talking?"* I was short of words! Do I still need to ease myself into it? And she gave me an emphatic **YES** and also showed me how to ease myself into it, and I'm going to share my information with you.

Easing yourself into dirty talking is quite simple, but it requires the use of all your sense organs. What do I mean? When you want to start dirty talking, you will look like a stranger if you don't talk by addressing all sense organs. For instance, instead of just saying, *"I love your meat,"* or *"caress me,"* you could also say, *"I love the way you sound when I suck you"* or *"you taste yummy"* or *"you look hot"* or *"you smell nice, baby"* or *"you are setting me on fire, baby."*

If you check out the dirty talks above, you will discover that each sentence made use of a different sense organ, and this allows you to slip into dirty talking mode because there will be lots of dirty talks available to you. I know this isn't easy, and you are most likely used to dirty talking with two sense organs, that are, *your sight, "you look delicious, babe. Can I eat you?" and your touch, "I love it when you fondle with my breast."* However, to dirty talk easily and continually have ideas that will spice up your sexual life, **you got to do what you got to do.** You need to learn to use all senses because it leads to one of the keys to introducing dirty talk to yourself and reviving your sex life.

Another way to ease yourself into dirty talk is by informing your partner about the talk. Tell them beforehand that you want to add a little spark to the sexual experience. This way, he would inform you if what you say is lovely or offensive. I know you might be scared of drawbacks, and you hate rejection, especially if it is coming from your lover. However, if you guys do talk about sex before, it should be easy for you to tell him you want to try dirty talking. Most times, the reason why you don't ease into dirty talking is that your mind seeks to protect your image; it creates a sexual barrier that prevents your partner from having a bad image that comes from messing it all up. However, if you want to be a dirty talk goddess, then you need to go over this barrier, and the best way to do that is by talking to your lover about dirty talking. This way, he won't be caught by surprise, and your image is preserved.

If it is comfortable with you, make a list of safe dirty talks in your mind by asking your lover what he thinks about them. For instance, you can ask him what he feels about spanking you. If he is okay with it, then you can tell him, *"spank me, baby"* when the time comes, and his reaction will make you happy, or he doesn't like the idea, and you strike it out and try again later. If you are still finding it uneasy to dirty talk, take a deep breath, look into his face, remember his consent, remember his love and trust, and I tell you, dirty talking will become ABC to you.

These steps are the easiest ways to ease you into dirty talking. You just need your senses and an understanding with your partner, which will make dirty talking easy, ensure that you are not short of words, and also preserve your image.

The Do's and Don'ts of dirty talk

When you want to dirty talk, here are what you must do and what you mustn't do.

Do say to him that he is powerful and good. Do you know that nothing has more effect on a man than sexy compliments? If you don't, now you know. So, when you enter the dirty talking mode, especially during sex, praise him. You can say stuff like, *"Oh baby, you are strong. I like that."* This will heighten the sexual pleasure, and your dirty talk will have the desired effect.

Using defamatory words is highly prohibited. Don't try it. Admittedly, some words have sound effects on your partner, and some are just plain offensive. These defamatory words, although acceptable to some, are disgusting and a huge turn off to others. Examples of these words include **whore, slave, slut, etc**. These words create a self-esteem security alert instead of intensifying sexual pleasure. So, if you plan to enjoy dirty talking, do it away from these words because they might blow your chances of being a dirty talker from the first day. If you love these words, ask your partner for consent, but don't push it because there are other words you can use instead of defamatory words.

Don't ever tell your partner to shut it. This is the last thing that should ever happen to you. It is an unacceptable mistake. Imagine that your partner tells you to shut up when you tried to dirty talk. Would you love it? Would you still be turned on? I doubt that. So, don't do it. Even if the way they talk sounds funny or nasty, stay calm. I know you might be angry at his comments, but don't react when you're upset. Try to wait until after sex and then talk to him about it. You might be surprised that he didn't mean to hurt you and most probably heard the line from a porn video, which isn't real. If you can't continue the sex, stop it immediately and talk about his comments. But, it's wrong to tell him to shut it. Please don't do it.

Ensure that you scream his name. If you don't know, I should tell you. No guy doesn't love you screaming his name. If you can't yell it, maybe because of lousy neighbors, then say it loudly. It gives him the impression that you are his, and he is yours. So, as many times as possible, say his name. It goes a long way and has more effects than saying, *"I want you to fuck me harder."*

Finally, **Don't use medical words.** If you check every dirty talk dictionary, you will hardly find medical words that talked about sensitive human body parts. This is because these words are enemies to sexual pleasure. Why would you say, *"I want to suck your penis" when you can say, "I want to suck your dick/cock". Why would you say, "My breasts need your touch" when you can say," My boobs/tits need your touch."* Think about it. Which one makes more sense as a dirty talk? I know you have traveled the world and gathered various educational experiences. But, when it comes to dirty talking, leave your certificates at the bedroom door. It is called dirty talk because the words aren't clean. So, drop medical words describing the body parts because it's not sexy; start using those dirty words.

After you have eased yourself into dirty talking and are familiar with the Do's and Don'ts, then you need to know how to get comfortable because when you are nervous, you will most likely fail.

The first step to getting comfortable is to **know the right way to describe your physique.** You need to understand how you want to be described, and this will be a guide to your lover, and you won't be a victim of bad, dirty talks. It is important to know how you want to be addressed; as a slut? Baby? Or do you want your body part to be called vagina, pussy, cochie, or even vulva? If you know how you want to be described, it will make you comfortable and less scared of a reduction in your self-esteem.

You need to answer this: how best do you want your actions to be described? It is imperative. What is that word that you find sexy? For instance, I love it when my man uses the term *"dive"* it immediately turns me on, and in a few seconds, I'm wet waiting for the diver. You might love it when your man says, *"I want to pound you."* and it is different from *"I want to fuck you."* so, discover your best word and let your lover know.

Talk about the past, present, and future. Do you remember the secrets to becoming successful at sexting in chapter 1? All you need to do is apply it. When you are confused and blank on what to say during the action, use those secrets to get comfortable. Reminisce your sexual activities with him, prompt him, tease him, and foreshadow future sexcapades.

Simply put, tell him to remember what he did on that day which made you cum so hard; tell him to do it again. Tell him how you want to suck his cock. Ask him if he likes the way you suck him. Telling him how you want to try a fantasy the next time you guys fuck.

Don't limit yourself to the bedroom. Another reason why some women are uncomfortable with dirty talk is that they only do it in the four walls of the bedroom. So, be comfortable to talk about it everywhere. Let him know how much you miss the action even if you lasted the standard times of a football match the night before. This will make you comfortable, and you won't need to start racking your head for words when you are in the bedroom.

Finally, you can also get comfortable with dirty talking if you practice with friends. Don't get me wrong; this doesn't mean you should sleep with your male besties, just harmless talk. Pick someone free with you and talk about everything until you find it comfortable to tell your man some dirty talks.

How to find your seductive voice?

Most women don't dirty talk and prefer to moan during sex because they are scared of sounding normal rather than sexy. They are worried that the sound of their voice will crack them up or turn them off. Are you one of these women? Yes, or No, it is best known to you. However, relax and learn these easy ways to make your voice seductive and sexy.

Speak using a deep range: have you tried talking with a deep voice? I know you haven't. Speaking this way gives your partner the idea that you are calm, and you have got control over what you are doing. On the other hand, when you don't express yourself, it gives your partner the idea that you are nervous and worried about your performance. I know this action might seem hard, but as the famous adage goes, *"PRACTICE MAKES PERFECT!"*

Deeply talking doesn't mean that you should speak like a man. It just means that you should speak in a calm and relaxed voice. Don't rush the words out of your mouth; keep it soft. This doesn't mean that you should whisper continuously, but you just need to watch the volume because it goes a long way in determining if your voice would be sexy or not. Lowering volume levels on some dirty talks and even ordinary words have a sexy effect on your lover. Try this: say, *"what's your plan tonight"* then reduce the volume of your voice when you say, *"mine is free, and I would be happy to keep you company."* I want you to watch for the reactions it would have on your test subject. If it clicks, then you have started your journey as a seductress, and you just need to master the voice and spice it up with some sexy actions. However, if it doesn't work for you, it just means you haven't found the voice or your body language and words are contradictory. I know the road might be bittersweet at first, but with perseverance and practice, you can be a veteran seductress, an impressive dirty talker, and your partner would be in constant awe of you because you will rock his world.

Fact: do you know that it is scientifically proven that using your sexy/seductive voice has a terrific effect not only on your lover but anyone? A study carried out by Dr. Sarah Hughes, an assistant professor in the Department of Psychology, on twenty women who used a calm, deep, seductive voice in talking to twenty men who were total strangers showed that the men wanted to know and get associated with them. Their voice quickly affected them, making them subject to their seductive advances. Now tell me, why won't you have a hot voice?

SUMMARY

Dos and Don'ts of Dirty Talk

- ✓ Tell your partner that he is powerful and strong
- ✓ Never use defamatory words
- ✓ Never tell your partner to shut up
- ✓ Make sure you scream your partner's name
- ✓ Never Use Medical terms/words

How you want your actions to be described

- ✓ Make sure you use sexy words to make your dirty talk enjoyable
- ✓ Do not limit dirty talk to the bedroom
- ✓ You can practice some dirty talk words with friends to become proficient

How to find your seductive voice?

- ✓ Speak using a deep range

Chapter 4: Meet the Talk

The Dirty Talk

In all spheres of life, communicating with someone builds a special connection between you and the person. This, in its entirety, is also the case with sexual activities. However, it is okay if you face some hurdles, which will seem overwhelming when trying to dirty talk because the ability to fuck and talk is a skill that requires practice and courage. Our societal configuration about sex and its related activities remains a significant barrier to higher participation of people because a more substantial part of our global populace sees any sexual practice as an action that shouldn't be freely spoken of, an act only meant for the bedroom. However, this is 2020, and its high time we destroyed these barriers and improved the sex life of not only us but also generations to come.

This chapter will be focused generally on dirty talk, and it will also cover some dirty talk fails so that you can avoid making these mistakes, which has affected other dirty talkers.

Typically, if you ask anyone about the meaning of dirty talk, most replies would be, *"it is a skill used to intensify sex and heighten pleasure."* However, have you ever wondered why this skill, as essential and useful as it is in preserving your marriage and keeping the sexual spark, isn't revealed to you by your parents or relative? The answer isn't farfetched. When I was a little girl, a significant part of my daily knowledge acquisition is that talking about sexual actions is wrong; anyone who talks about it is bad; and this registered in my mind as I grew up. My parents followed this rule, my grandparents followed suit, and I'm sure my great grandparents, although I didn't meet her, would have believed and followed that rule. I know I'm not the first girl to be taught this way in the world, and surely, I won't be the last. This knowledge becomes the first law in our sexual commandments as kids, buried deeply in our subconscious, making us strive to be good girls and boys to our sexual partners when the time is right. We begin to speak to ourselves, *"only bad girls talk about sexual acts."* *"No good boy will talk about the sexual act."* This ideology is carried into adulthood, and even worse, into marriage, and instead of dirty talking, we create different types of moan for various heights of sexual pleasure, and when this starts to fail, and the sex isn't enjoyable as it used to, we try to save it by seeking advice which will lead to someone telling us about dirty talks. However, it becomes hard to reconfigure the mind because of the good girl image, which has been preserved for over 20 years and is in danger of extinction. Also talking about sexual acts will activate the bad girl mode, which makes you uncomfortable, especially if someone of authority like a mom or dad is available to dish out words against you if they hear that you are now a dirty talker.

Then, after reading lots of articles and watching videos on dirty talking, you realize that you have been wrong all along, and you see dirty talk as a must-have skill. You find out that moaning and not talking put your partner in an awkward position because he has to pleasure you without knowing what he is doing right, what you like, and what is turning you off. He is blank, and since he isn't telepathic, he is unable to read you, which leaves him frustrated and causes a significant decline in sexual pleasure and performance. Then, you decide to meet the talk, but you are plagued with various issues because you didn't start early. You get confused because many self-help books on sex will urge you to maintain open lines of communication in bed while other sex guidebooks will inform you to keep your lips sealed *"minimize talk during intercourse because this can distract your lover and ruin the mood "*, resulting in a soft dick.

So, which of these books is preaching the truth? My advice is that you need to understand your partner; this will make you know when to give to him hot and when just to whisper one at a time.

While the goal is to give your partner the mind-blowing sex that will make him run back home after work for round two, having a good choice of words is crucial. The wrong set of words with the right intentions could distract your lover's thoughts, and sometimes, yours from the moment. It's the choice of words we use that is the difference between awesome or awful sex. Let's check out some dirty talk fails.

Dirty talk fails

Like I earlier said, word choice determines whether you are going to enjoy the sex as much as you want. However, using the wrong words, even if your intents are right, would lead to distractions and equally disrupt the full flow of sexual pleasure between you and your lover. Let look at some real-life examples of dirty talk fails.

"Stay put, baby. I want to give you a nice kiss."

Nasty? No **X**

Instructive? Yes ✓

Sexy? Not really **X**

Disruptive? Surely ✓

This statement looks okay, right? However, it is a fault in some areas. It leaves little to the imagination, pauses the action, and reduces the pleasure. After that kiss (if it eventually happens), it becomes hard to reignite the fire. Let's look at another example with the same meaning.

"I want to kiss your sexy lips, baby."

Nasty? No **X**

Instructive? Yes ✓

Sexy? Absolutely ✓

Disruptive? No! ✓

Two words, same meaning, and different sexual effect.

Let's look at another one

"Baby, don't cum before me."

Nasty? No ✓

Instructive? Absolutely ✓

Sexy? Not really ✗

Disruptive? Yes! ✗

As much as possible, try not to make this mistake. This statement, as small and insignificant as it seems, is having an uncertain meaning. Imagine that your man is giving you the best strokes, enjoying himself, and also believing that you are enjoying it too. Then you drop this bombshell, Wow! The meaning is that you are not close to orgasm. I know you might want to say, *"but I wasn't close to orgasm, why shouldn't I say it."* However, the issue isn't you being far from orgasm but how you say it. Try this: *"oh, yes!" Say his name," don't stop; I'm going to cum."* It's the same message, but which will have a better result? I leave it to you to decide.

"Fill me with your cum, let me make babies for you."

Nasty? Not at all ✗

Instructive? Very ✓

Sexy? A little bit ✓

Disruptive? Powerfully **X**

If you are a married couple, then this might not affect you. However, this statement isn't advised if you don't know your lover's intentions, and you are still unmarried. When you are making love with your partner who doesn't want to have kids yet, and you say this statement, all sexual energy dissipates, defense mechanism kicks in, and his reaction would most likely be to say, *"What?"* And quickly fish out his cock from your pussy, spoiling the fun. So, if you aren't sure that your partner wants babies, just say, *"I want your cum in me"* or *"fill me with your cum."* It will have a good effect on him and reduce the baby scare.

Although fails aren't good and they adversely affect sexual pleasure, you can't entirely avoid them, but you can reduce them. Sometimes what you think is regular dirty talking would be quite offensive to your partner. But don't be discouraged when it happens. Always remember that you learn by your experiences. Thus, I implore you to dirty talk endlessly with your partner because it is the easiest way to maintain sexual tension and keep him thinking about you all day long.

I had a friend, let's call her Paula.

Paula, while having sex, told her man, "oh babe, you are so much better than I thought you'd be. Fuck me harder."

I bet you just laughed too. Let's admit it, Paula wanted to give a sexy compliment; she wanted to let him know that he blew her mind, that he is a good fuck. But she blew it by telling him she thought he would be crap, and he changed her thoughts. Would that sexual experience end with the required tension? I leave that to you to decide.

SUMMARY

- ✓ Communicating with someone builds a special connection between you and the person

- ✓ Our societal configuration about sex and its related activities remains a significant barrier to higher participation of people in dirty talk

- ✓ An excellent choice of word is the difference between awesome and bad in dirty talk

- ✓ Understand your partner

Chapter 5: Walk the Talk

In this chapter, we will be taking the first step towards becoming an expert at talking dirty, and that is - understanding your style and your partner's. Different strokes for different folks; this can also be said to be the case with dirty talking.

One of the fundamentals of dirty talking is about understanding what works for you. What types of words are you biased too? Do you like the use of medical terms, do you prefer slang, or do you just like borderline nasty!

The good news is that the process of figuring out what works for you or your partner is pretty much the same, and if applied correctly, you can also figure out what works for other people.

The Process

Dirty talk isn't for everyone; some people just can't manage to pull it off without laughing because frankly, they find understanding the type of words that their partners respond to daunting and borderline impossible; *What if he doesn't like it? What if it's insulting? How far is too far?* These are genuine questions. Not every woman is comfortable with being called a Slutty *Bitch!* And contrary to popular beliefs, not every man is comfortable with being called Daddy, *or* in some cases, *Zaddy*! – I found this hilarious. So how do you figure out what to say? The steps are as simple as 1, 2, 3, and they work for you, your partner, and quite frankly, anyone.

Step 1–Observe

Everyone loves compliments! This is a fact. Everyone likes to be reminded of the nice suit they have on, the hair that they put effort into making, their beautiful polished shoes, the dress that they spent 2 hours picking, their matching shoes and purse. Everyone loves compliments. But most of all, everyone loves honest compliments. Don't tell me I have the best dentition on the planet when I know I have the worst! And don't tell me I have great hair when my hairline is receding!

Everyone has some sort of insecurity that they are not comfortable with talking about at any time, and they definitely won't be comfortable with it being said during dirty talking.

Nobody enjoys talking about their insecurities

Sure, it is good to help your partner overcome their insecurities, but there are a time and a place for it, and *"dirty talk time"* isn't *"supportive partner time."*

Take your time to study your partner carefully. Every human on the planet has one thing or more that they love about themselves. Something as insignificant as liking the way their pinky toe looks – I've seen all sorts – it matters!

All you need do is observe them, and it comes out naturally, and you could go a step further by having a playful chat with them about it. Tease them, or play a game and ask them, *"what do you like the most about yourself?"* You'd be surprised at some of the responses you'll get. Take your time to understand the little things. Take note of the little things, *that one side of her face that she takes selfies of the most, that part of his body he doesn't mind talking about, the hairdo she's repeated twice in a month, the efforts he puts into having well-groomed beards.* These are just examples of different things that you should observe.

Beyond the physical, you could take a step to understand their habits and preference. Habits are incredibly accurate in determining what your partner likes. Forming a habit takes constant repetition and time. In most scenarios, no one continually repeats what they do not love until it becomes habitual. Preferences, on the other hand, are what they sound like, preference! Where they like going, *What football or basketball team does he like? what's her favorite genre of literature? What type of video games does he play? What's her favorite place to be? What pet name does she like?* These are sample questions that demonstrate a preference.

The importance of this step will be seen later, but do take note that it is of the utmost importance.

Step 2 – Words and Action

Proceeding to step 2 means you already have a lock on pretty much how your partner is. You're aware of their likes, dislikes, their favorite physical features, or their favorite place to be. You pretty much know them. Step 2 requires a bit of technicality, and it entails finding the words that best *communicate* what you learned about them. The term *"best"* that I used connotes finding the *nicest, politest, and the most precise words or phrases* that describe what you learned about them and taking action.

When I first wrote out these steps for my friend, she found step 2 the most challenging and quite possibly so. Different words have different effects on people when used in different ways, and what exactly do I mean by actions? Here is an example

A man that practiced step 1, taking time to observe his wife, asked questions, and learns the things she likes and hates:

She likes her round butt

She likes her job

She hates her small belly fat

She loves her kids

She likes swimming

She likes being called a baby.

This is a fair list, not being too good, or bad either. The question is, *how do I compliment her love for swimming? Or her job? The* answer is you don't! You take action! You take her to the pool for a swim, or you help with the critical document she brought from work.

When you help someone do what they like, they tend to feel happier and comfortable around, and it gently eases them into being comfortable to say things they usually wouldn't. This is a perfect place to be. You want your partner to be very comfortable around you for you to ease them into talking dirty with you gently.

Verbal compliments also go a long way in making your partner feel good about themselves but before complimenting them, understand the type of *adjectives* they are comfortable with... maybe they like a conservative one, perhaps they like using medical terms, maybe she prefers the word *breast* to *boobs* or *mammary gland,* that would be up to you to find out.

If you are unsure of the types of words to use, and you are not interested in going through step 1 again, you could try using generic words and make the compliments just barely decent enough.

Here is an example; we will be making use of the results the man we earlier mentioned got from his wife

She likes her round butt

She likes her job

She hates her small belly fat

She loves her kids

She likes swimming

She likes being called babe

Let us assume he wants to compliment her butt; he could go in any direction

You've got a sweet ass babe

Your butt looks, nice babe

You look nice in those trousers, babe

These are all compliments that refer to the nice overall shape of her butt in decreasing order of how raunchy they get. When you are not aware of what a person likes, or you know they tend to hate sexual things, the safest bet is to go with the least suggestive compliment only.

The mistake some people might make is assuming that *"safe"* compliments like this are annoying, but that couldn't be more wrong. Generalized compliments create room for imagination, and they tend to be perfect conversation starters.

A well-used *"That new top looks good on you"* creates a sense of intrigue, and subconsciously, questions like *"Was he looking at my boobs?" "Is he complimenting my waist?" "Does he like my body frame? "* and a whole lot more begins to creep into the mind.

With the person being complimented not sure of the intent, it creates a sense of intrigue and mystery for the person complimenting, a perfect way to kick start a new relationship or solidify an old one.

Step 3–Test-Run

The final step is the application! There is no one way to dirty talk, but with steps 1 and 2 perfected, by step 3, your partner would pretty much be excited whenever you are around. You took your time and observed them, and also made compliments that mattered, and by now, you should already start noticing subtle but exciting changes in your relationship.

Before you utter that first naughty *word*, ensure that your partner is in a place of comfort, and gently roll it out. Keep nasty and naughty to a minimum, and slowly ease them into it. Get comfortable, slowly seducing your partner with suggestive words. The change could be as subtle as changing "want" to "need" or changing that "sweetheart" to "babe" or changing the word "dick" to "cock". Slowly but surely, they get comfortable hearing it, and you will get comfortable saying it.

There is no shortcut to mastering the art of dirty talking. You will need to try over and over, but you will mostly be fine. You observed them, and you have an idea of the words they are comfortable hearing.

Seduction

Most of the time, with couples and lovers I have counseled, they all complain about *hitting a specific wall! "How do I make my partner want to have sex with me?" "How do I seduce my partner?"*

I always end up having to explain the art of seduction, and I will include that here. After rigorously putting effort into steps 1 and 2, you finally know a lot about your partner, and your partner is always excited to be with you, but how do you initiate sex? How do you make yourself irresistible to your partner?

Lots of books have been written on seduction, too many to count, and if you are reading this book, chances are you have come across one or two of such books. But if you haven't, don't fret; you will find this section useful. To make things easy, I'll be looking at two unique ways of seduction that have proven most effective.

Verbal Seduction

Contrary to popular belief, verbal seduction isn't just dirty talking; it goes way beyond that. The two most essential things in verbal seduction are the *tone of your voice* and your *choice of words.*

Your tone comes down to how you sound and how you pronounce your words. Not every man is born with that cool deep voice that just calms the nerves when you hear it, and quite frankly, not every woman has the *voice of a nightingale,* but you could learn to sound relaxed or gentle.

I always recommend that you start by making a simple voice recording of yourself saying any random words. Play it back and listen to how it sounds. Be sincere with yourself and ask, *"Do I talk too fast, or too slow?" Do I have a weird way of pronouncing certain words?" Am I audible?"* If any of these questions answer yes, get to work on fixing it. Keep practicing different speech mannerisms you are comfortable with until all the questions answer no! Your choice of words matters a lot with verbal seduction. Avoid slang when trying to seduce your partner unless it's a unique word that you both share.

With verbal seduction, *simple trumps complex every time.* Keep your vocabulary simple while being mindful of your tone. If you want to introduce dirty talk in a conversation, keep it to a minimum, and gradually increase the intensity. And if your partner seems uncomfortable with the words, stop! And you start finally applying verbal seduction with your partner; don't overwhelm them by suddenly changing how you talk. Slowly and gradually change it, pace yourself, and in no time, you will have your partner craving every inch of your body.

Aesthetic Seduction

I find aesthetic seduction or seduction of the five senses the most fascinating and exciting way of seduction. If you can successfully seduce all five senses of a person, you technically own them. But being successful at this takes years of practice, and I believe you don't have that long, so I came up with these three tested and trusted tips.

Look the part

Perhaps the most important of the five senses is sight. A lot of the daily interaction we make requires that we see the person before proceeding to any other thing, and the key to seducing your partner's sight is to look good. Looking good is beyond just clothes; your actions also affect your look. Feel comfortable in what you wear. Avoid overly flashy clothes and dress *for the season!* Don't wear summer clothes in the winter or winter clothes during the spring.

Your physique also matters a lot. If you are not comfortable with how you look or feel, join that yoga class or join that gym. Staying healthy is very vital to looking good. Not only do you look more physically appealing, but you also feel confident.

ACT THE PART

While looking good helps a lot with aesthetic seduction, you need to learn to act the part. Nobody wants a snob, and no matter how good you look, if you don't act right, you won't be seducing anybody, let alone your partner; you'd most likely be doing the opposite.

Acting the part requires self-discipline and consistency! To perform the part, you first have to get busy! *Yes, get busy!* We tend to want to always be around people we like, and there is nothing wrong with that, but with seduction, that would be a wrong move. If you are always around and available, you come off as *needy and jobless,* and quite frankly, *uninteresting.* Seduction and neediness cannot co-exist. Think of it this way, if you aren't always around, then the little times you are around would matter more.

But beyond making yourself scarce, you also have to effectively make use of the times you are with your partner. Send subtle signals, flirt a little. Depending on the social situation, you could touch their arms gently or shoulders while maintaining eye contact.

Flirt with your eyes! I can't state this enough! The human eyes are very *powerful tools* that can communicate *desire* without you uttering a single word. When making eye contact, fix your gaze on their eyes, and slowly pull away.

Never be in haste to look elsewhere. A trick that works effectively is to vividly imagine what you want to do to them while looking them straight in their eyes, and your eyes will do the rest.

Also, no matter the scenario, loud outbursts and swearing are a no go. Always stay calm and cool-headed, no matter the situation you find yourself, and add a bit of witty humor. Humor plays a significant role in making you look appealing. If you can make your partner smile, the process is 30% complete.

Breathe

Beyond just looking good and acting cool when you're trying to seduce your partner, please yourself! Have fun! In your attempt to seduce them, remember that your mental health remains the most important. Have fun! Learn to enjoy your own company! Pick up a hobby! Do the things you love! People are most attractive when they do the things; they love the most. If you're going too fast, pause and take a breather. The key to becoming a master seducer is to enjoy the process of seduction truly and not seeing it as monotonous. Don't get too cut up in it. Be playful, and finally, give it time. *Seduction is art!* Art should not be rushed. So, while you expect the best results in the shortest time possible, are realistic with your expectations and, from time to time, re-evaluate your position, and learn on the go, and things will turn out fine.

These three tips have worked countless times for me, my friends, and any other person that I have advised on the subject: both male and female, and if you follow through, you'll have your partnerdrooling *in* no time.

Seduction is practically the euphoria of the passion itself, while seduction isn't similar to sex, it's the medium that preserves all sexual pleasure essential for a mind-blowing sexual experience.

SUMMARY

- ✓ The three significant steps in becoming competent at dirty talk are, observe, words and action, and the test-run.
- ✓ *"observe" is* one of the first and most important steps, and if done right, it lays a perfect foundation for the remaining steps.
- ✓ Words and action is the second step, and it solely focuses on different ways of getting your partner comfortable around you.
- ✓ Test-run is the last step. You put all the information you've learned to the test and try again if you fail.
- ✓ Master the art of seduction.
- ✓ Voice tone, diction, and choice of words matter the most in verbal seduction.
- ✓ Aesthetic seduction accounts for how you look, act, and the type of vibe you give.

Chapter 6:
Live the Talk

Introducing it to your partner

When I meet with someone who wants to dirty talk but doesn't know how to go about it, 9 out of 10 would always ask a significant question, *"how do I introduce it to my partner?"* Each time, I always explain this question and proffer ideas and solutions to it. Let's face it, learning how to dirty talk isn't just for you to feel good, but you also want to give your partner those moments that would make him/her say, *"whoa."* So, let me ask you a question. Are you worried about how you can introduce dirty talk to your lover? If you are, get a book and pen because you will need to jot things down. If you aren't or you already dirty talk but are looking for that extra spark that will make your sex life explosive, then you also need to jot something down because this chapter covers ways to introduce dirty talk to your lover and additional details to get him in the mood.

First, you need to realize that the words and actions that get you into the mood; may not affect your man. This is why understanding your partner before introducing the talk is highly essential. Ask yourself, *"Do I understand my lover?"* If yes, then raising the talk would be effortless. Otherwise, then you need to know your partner. You are wondering how to understand that partner? Check out the previous chapter!

Most new couples and even long-time lovers who aren't used to freakiness always find it hard to introduce dirty talk to their lovers because telling your partner that you want to try dirty words, especially when your sex is all about silence, may seem daunting, awkward and overwhelming. However, this shouldn't be the case because it's relatively easy to introduce the talk. Here are easy ways to introduce the talk.

Guide

An excellent way to start the introduction of dirty talk to your partner is to act as a guide. This is the easiest way to begin your journey. Guide your partner by taking the talk a step at a time. One major problem is that most people only want to start the talk in the bedroom; however, for your introduction to be successful, it's best to begin guiding when you aren't fucking. For instance, if your partner isn't a freaky one, start the talk with words that aren't borderline nasty. Here are some ideas for you.

"Whoa, don't you look handsome" (don't forget a smile and a badass sexy look.)

"I want you." (I lick my lips when I do this)

"Nice butt!" (spank a little)

"You are so freaking hot!"

"You smell good; do you taste yummy too?"

The words shouldn't be porn star quality; all you need is the right smile and attitude. The effect and that of an explicit expression are the same. Watch closely - note your partner's reactions to the talk. If he loves it, then you can begin to take it up a notch. However, if there is no reciprocity, then you need to move to the second introduction approach.

Talk

The second way of introduction is Talking. When your partner doesn't respond to your mild dirty talks, then you need to talk. Pick a time to have a good discussion about your love for dirty talk. You shouldn't talk when your partner is tired, stressed, or when he is just home from work. Talk when he is calm, healthy, happy, and you aren't having sex.

Talk about it, what he wants, the no-go-areas, etc. I know talking about anything sexual might look seemingly impossible for you. However, without it, you will continue to enjoy the surface and wouldn't be able to tap into the real meaning of "Good Sex."

Talking to your lover about sex is the gateway to the best sexual experience

Even if the guiding approach was successful for you, it is equally important to talk about the talk to prevent situations of dirty talk fails. Hence, before the bedroom action, it's crucial to identify the good talks and the ones you never want to use. Are you wondering how to start? Let me give you an approach.

Praise

Start by talking about the amount of pleasure you get from sex with him or her. You could say, *"Babe, before I met you, my sex life was in shambles, I never experienced _____, and I was always in_____, but after I met you, you rocked my world and my sex life boomed! I experienced ___, and all I want is that it should never end!"* (Your partner would most likely be grinning, happy, and also curious because he/she knows there's more to come.

Introduce

After heaping those praises on your partner, then it's time to talk about the talk. It's like pitching an idea, so it should be top-notch. Inform him/her why dirty talk is an undiscovered trick that must be done (chapter 1 covered everything you need for this) then start to ask him/her questions about their preferences. Note that the person you are talking to isn't a stranger; hence, being formal isn't allowed. Be funny, severe, yet playful. Note down his/her preference(s) and tell him yours. Does he like his sex organ addressed as a penis? Dick? Stick? or Rod? Does she like it when you call her sexual organ vagina? Pussy? Cunt? or Vulva? This plus many more words, is the information you need to know. Register them in your head.

Complement

Finally, talk about those sweet moments. Complement your lover for a particular sex position that leaves you panting and filled with pleasure. Talk about precious times and funny moments. Here are some ideas.

"You know you are bad, right? You found out I love when you suck my breast and fuck, and you won't stop doing it."

"The way you moan when I suck you is funny; you sound like a ____" (add a good laugh which will most likely be followed by a playful argument.)

In the end, you and your lover will be happy, laughing, and you will have created a dirty talk atmosphere with your lover.

However, if you still struggle with creating the conversation, then you can wait for moments such as when you both are seeing an X-rated scene where actors dirty talk or listening to a song, and you quickly say, *"dirty talk in bed is exciting, don't you think?"* This will ease you into the conversation, and your lover will open up to you. Also, you can use the opportunity to ask what dirty talk your lover would like to hear during sex. It will allow you to know if *"I want you"* would do the trick or you need to be borderline nasty with words like, *"cum in my pussy."*

Always remember that your desires and kinks are things you shouldn't be nervous about, and you should be free to inform your lover about them. However, if, during attempts to introduce the talk, you realize that your partner isn't comfortable with it, you shouldn't force it. Albeit you will feel disappointed because you want to hear those sexy words and your partner isn't interested. In this case, using the various techniques of dirty talk could come in handy when you seek to find a balance between you and your partner. It gives you the pleasure and also ensures that your partner does what he/she is comfortable with.

The big, then the small technique is quite simple. When you introduced the talk, and you meet a brick wall instead of a smile, try something smaller. For instance, if my lover tells me dirty talking isn't for him, I don't argue. However, during sex, I whisper some words in his ears. Soft dirty talks like, *"hmmm, just like that." "Oh, that feels so good!" "Please, don't stop."* Am I dirty talking? Yes! Did he realize I'm dirty talking? Maybe or maybe not.... But, most times, I hear moans escape his lips instead of *"shut up,"* and another time, he gave me a shocker. When I whispered, *"hmmm, just like that,"* he replied, *"you like that?"* Although he isn't a fan of dirty talking, he talked because I substituted some big action, "dirty talk" for a smaller one, "whispering" and in a short while, the reign of the talk began.

Sometimes, your lover will tell you that dirty talk is a taboo and wouldn't want to do it at all. Surprisingly, some even say things like, *"I will only dirty talk in death!" "Over my dead body would I dirty talk!"* Hence, once you realize your partner isn't keen on dirty talking ideas, leave it be. Better, you can ask your partner to include more moans in the sexual experience, adding those *"hmmms," "whoa", "arrggh",* and other kinds of sound also improve and intensify sexual pleasure. Maybe your lover isn't interested in the idea of dirty talking because he/she lacks knowledge of dirty words. Then, you need to assure them that you will assist and make their learning process stress-free and sweet.

All that's required to teach your partner the talk is to ensure that your dirty talks include more questions than statements. Instead of saying, *"fuck me,"* you should say, *"Baby, do you want to fuck me?" "What would you want to do to my body?" "How do you want to be sucked?"* Why questions are better than statements are because it prompts your lover to give you an answer. I bet you don't want to say, *"Oh, fuck me"* and hear your lover say, *"okay,"* so ask those questions, slowly at first, and encourage the replies with some loud moans or sexy body movements. This way, there is no need for your partner to start brain-scanning for some cool dirty talks for a good sexual conversation.

Finally, although it is an excellent call to talk about everything in a relationship, don't expect it to be favorable at all times. Dirty talk introductions aren't always a success, and an early realization of this will allow you to brace yourself for what is to come. However, talking about the talk with your lover will always remain top in the list of smart moves for introducing the dirty talk. This way, they would reveal their wants to you, and you may be surprised that a cold lover of yours is a diehard fan of talking dirty, which will open doors for sexual adventures.

Let me give you a bonus...

The predictable lover

One of the worst drawbacks of talking dirty is being a predictable lover. Remember this, every naughty word that leaves a girl squirting or a guy shooting his load are most times completely unfiltered, raw, and fresh. These words portray the exact feelings at that particular moment; they are words that connect to the lovers at the highest level, words produced from instincts. Simply put, when introducing the talk to your lover, to have the desired effect, be unpredictable, and let your comments show a connection between you and your lover.

Becoming unpredictable is easy, and you shouldn't let it overwhelm you. There is a straightforward rule you need to follow.

Don't use the words that turned him on yesterday; go by what he responds to today

In short, how your lover responds to your dirty talk, not a pre-planned rehearsed list of words. If your lover responded to *"oh, baby"* the last time, and if he surprisingly responds to *"hmmm"* today, build your castle around it using words having *"hmmm"*. If, after a while, he isn't responding anymore to *"hmmm,"* stop using it, and try out something new from the list of words you know he is comfortable with. Don't be predictable by using the words you used yesterday and two days ago.

Turning up the mood

In the first chapter, where we look at the psychology behind the dirty talk, we discussed that the mood of you and your partner is vital for any dirty talk to succeed, and we also looked at one way to create the right mood, that is, *the power of date nights.*

In introducing the talk to your partner, do it in the right mood puts the odds in your favor. However, if there is no time for date nights or you are not a fan of outdoor entertainment, then how do you create the mood? It is quite effortless to turn up the mood using these tips.

Erotica

I've met a couple of women who wouldn't dare handle any erotica book, and it always amazes me. Perhaps they do not know that erotica books help sex and also turn up the mood in the reader, maybe. Let's check out an expert opinion on the effect of erotica books.

At the seminar held on the Gold Coast regarding sexology, a renowned expert in sexuality named Kerrin Bradfield, while teaching on sex education, said thus:

"Apart from acting as a form of informal sex education, reading erotica can stimulate the imagination for fantasies, providing new ideas to help keep an intimate relationship exciting."

If you are a reader and your partner is equally one, pick up an erotica book and read together. It will broaden your imagination, successfully bury your lover in wild thoughts of you, which will build up the mood, and increase sexual tension. For instance, if you are a fan of sexual kinks, BDSM, and dirty talk, why not pick a book like the 50 Shades Trilogy; which will heighten the mood, make your partner want to try those kinks, and most likely lead to mind-blowing sex.

X-rated movies/porn

Typically, a significant percentage of the world population sees porn as something terrible, a taboo. However, if you are one of those, then you need to reconfigure your brain for the incoming information.

X-rated movies and porn videos have numerous benefits. However, we will be looking at the two that concern us, which are the ones that improve sex and help the sexual mood. Seeing raunchy movies helps in making way for a successful dirty talk introduction. For instance, if you are on the internet and you visit pornhub.com, try watching a video of Sarah Banks. She has a Master's and Ph.D. in dirty talking. Watch with your man and chip in comments like, *"Her dirty talk is awesome, I would love to try that."* Shots fired! His reaction would most likely be positive because he is in the mood.

If you see real porn action as a step over the line, get some pop-corn, some beer, and set the stage for a night of Netflix and Chilling. Watch movies like *Secretary, Swimming pool, Magic Mike, Love, Body heat,* which contain a lot of sex scenes with some nice dirty talking.

These movies will turn up the heat, and you will find your uptight lover loosen up, which will allow easy dialogue.

Let me give you a bonus for the girls

Cuddles

Apart from men who love to be the dominant one in a BDSM world, all other men love to cuddle. Press that ass to his crotch and wrap his hands around your breasts for a while. Wiggle the ass a bit, pretending to look for a more comfortable position and ask him about dirty talking. I bet you - the odds are in your favor, because your lover is now under your command.

Conclusively, it is always best to properly introduce the talk to your lover before taking it to the bedroom. Most men don't handle surprises well, so, to prevent a bedroom shocker or a laugh instead of a kiss, ensure that you introduce the talk to him.

*Khloe has always wanted to be a dirty talker, but she is still stumped on the best approach to introduce it to Drew without looking stupid. Should she use the babe, how would you describe my vulva technique or come out openly with **I want us to try talking DIRTY?** Now, she is anxious about being anxious when talking to him about it and is almost on the verge of living the rest of her life without the joy of talking dirty. Then, I gave her the same advice I just gave you, opened her eyes to these easy-peasy secrets, and ways to turn up the mood, which allows easy introduction. After raising the mood, a bit, and using the cuddle trick, she opened the floor for an easy introduction, and she got a positive result. Drew wasn't pissed, neither did he find her stupid. He was willing to try it out, and their sexual life skyrocketed! Would you let talking dirty introduction to your lover become a barrier to enjoying the benefits of talking dirty? I hope not!*

SUMMARY

How to introduce the talk

- ✓ Act as a guide
- ✓ Talk to your partner (guide, introduce, and complement)

Turning up the mood

- ✓ Erotica
- ✓ X-rated movies/porn
- ✓ Cuddles

Chapter 7: Live the Talk

In the Bedroom

If you want to take your man to a new height of climax that will write your name in gold on his heart, then learning and using the right technique is your best bet. It's the difference between average and mind-blowing sex. When I started dirty talking, after the first trial, my lover told me, *"I want you to talk dirty."* It came as a shocker, and I almost couldn't say a word because I didn't want to make mistakes, and I haven't discovered the techniques that will make me a General in dirty talking. Of course, that night, it ended in tears, and I knew I had to research further about dirty talk techniques, which I did and turned the tides in my favor.

Hence, this chapter covers dirty talk techniques to arouse your lover's senses in the bedroom and common mistakes to avoid when dirty talking. So, let's have at it.

Before sex, say what you want during sex, say what you like

An excellent technique to start talking dirty is to speak to your lover about your sexual wants or fantasies before the time your lover would fulfill it. During the act, be descriptive about what you like them to do to you.

Let's look at some examples

Here are a couple named Jane and Simon

Jane: *I want to ride you while you sit on a chair.*

Simon: *whoa, I want that too. I want you. (Before the sex, they've described what they wanted)*

Jane: *oh, fuck me harder.*

Simon: *play with my balls, babe.*

(During sex they are saying what they like.)

It's relatively easy, right?

What you want and what you like technique allows you to dirty talk easily. It ensures that you aren't faced with a brick wall, which will lead to numerous mistakes. All you have to do is voice out your wants and likes; how hard can it be?

You don't have to be borderline nasty to say your wants; neither will you be called a porn star if you voice your likes to your lover bearing in mind the limits of what you can say to him. If saying statements like *"I want your dick in me or make me yours"* seems raw to you, settle for something smaller, *"I need you"* has the same effect as wanting a dick, and you have successfully said what you want. You don't necessarily have to say, *"Fuck me harder,"* if it's not your preference. Using, *"I love how your hands feel on my body,"* will do the trick in telling your lover what you like.

Remember, the act of dirty talking must be quite descriptive; describe how you feel, how you like to be sucked, hugged, etc.—explaining everything paints that image in the mind of your lover and makes the dirty talk effective.

Gauge his reaction

When dirty talking, while the pleasure can be distracting, it's best you don't drift away. That moment, you are the detective, and your lover is the suspect. Watch his reaction to your words, gauge it. Do you feel his dick throb more when you mention a particular word? Exploit it. For instance, when you are having sex, and you see your lover overflow with energy whenever you say *"Ass,"* exploit it. Say,

"You love my ass, right?"

"My ass is yours."

"Spank that ass."

"Cum on my ass."

Take note, different sentences, with one word in common, the same effect on the lover. Gauge the reaction at all times. If you note a decline in sex drive after a comment, strike it out! Read those signals and signs emitting from your lover, and he will never forget those sexual moments.

Take charge

This doesn't mean you should dominate your lover unless perhaps he has a submissive fantasy that you want to fulfill. Taking charge simply means taking a director role in bed, becoming your lover's instructor.

Let's use Jane and Simon's example.

Jane: I want you to suck my breasts

Simon does it

Jane: oh, fuck me just like that

Simon continued the strokes with a smile

Jane: *I'm going to suck you till you blow your load.*

Simon lies down in anticipation

Simon: *babe, can I cum on your tits?*

Jane: *cum for me, baby.*

Jane is taking charge of the sex using dirty talks. But, does Simon know about this? I doubt he does. Is he enjoying it? Absolutely!

Taking charge allows you to slide into dirty talking easily. You only need to tell that partner what you want to do and what you want them to do without looking like Adolf Hitler.

These techniques arouse your lover's senses, allow you to talk without mistake, and ensure that you enjoy the act of dirty talking. I bet you are going to try them out today. Don't sleep on it!

Common mistakes to avoid while dirty talking

While mistakes are quite inevitable, it's essential to learn from other experiences to save oneself from future disgrace, embarrassing moments, and a nomination for the top 10 dirty talk mistakes of all time. Avoiding errors is vital in ensuring that you won't be slaughtered on the first day in to the quest for dirty talking.

Here are a couple of mistakes you must avoid;

Too much profanity

Although, talking dirty gets your lover in the mood, particularly in the four walls of the bedroom. However, where do you draw the line? At what point does your talks become offensive instead of arousing?

The first mistake people make when attempting to dirty talk or the first time is using the nastiest word that they can procure from their heads. It doesn't work that way!

While some lovers want to hear words like slut, whore, cum, dick, pussy, some detest it. They don't want to listen to it, and some perhaps want to hear those nasty words but not too often. Hence, when attempting to dirty talk, try to shy away from too much profanity or, better still, know what works best for your partner. This way, you would see if you need to 'up' your game, with some borderline nasty words or dirty talk like an angel without any profanity.

Let's look at an example.

Simon is a guy who likes dirty talk but hates profanity

Angelo likes profanity but not too much

Drew loves profanity

How do you dirty talk to the parties?

Tell Simon: I want to feel you inside me tonight.

Tell Angelo: I love sucking your dick.

Tell Drew: I'm your little sex toy; use me as your slut!

Imagine you used Drew's example for Simon or Angelo? Imagine that you used Simon's model for Angelo or Drew? The answers are the same. It will all go wrong, and you will be embarrassed. So, shy away from profanity or understand your lover to avoid this mistake.

Applying dirty talk from porn

A good percentage of women aren't fans of porn, but men are ardent lovers. However, this doesn't mean that they want you to go full porn star mode on them. Most dirty talks in porn aren't the way it seems, and mostly, they don't have that effect on your man in reality. So, drop it!

Talking non-stop

Talking too much kills the mood faster than lightning

I know talking dirty adds spice to sex life; I mean who and who doesn't want to add that spice? However, while it is good to speak, your lover would most likely get turned off if you just keep *talking* and *talking* and *talking*. I know you wish to take that talk up a notch; you want to open your vocal cords and pour out those words which will make your man's dick hard and going for a long time. However, I should inform you that dirty talk isn't just about the talk.

The only solution to stop talking non-stop is to watch your lover's reaction and gauge your sexual moments. Whenever you are dirty talking, and you discover there isn't any reciprocity from your lover, it could be that the words you're using aren't comprehensible. They lack the words or aren't really in the mood for dialogue. Whatever the reason may be, you mustn't talk all the way.

Calmly, read the body language between you and your lover.

Is he turned on?

Are there signs telling you to continue talking?

This will make you know if you should proceed and be all talk or stop talking and try another approach like asking questions.

Don't forget that dirty talk is more effective when adequately timed and delivered sexily. It can have a lasting effect on your lover when the right amount of words is said. However, too much spoils the fun. So, it is important to avoid excessive dirty talk.

Talking unbelievably

Don't forget that some dirty talk can easily be identified as a lie. For instance, telling that lover, *"Your dick is so big, fuck me"* when truthfully, it's below average won't make your lover feel high with pleasure. Most likely, you will get a frown and a turn-off.

It's always good to use exaggerations when talking about your lover. However, don't be extravagant with your exaggeration. If you truthfully address that lover who isn't happy about his dick size with a bit of hyperbole, it will improve their self-confidence and, in the long run, successfully kill the inhibition. However, if a majority of your dirty talk is laid on a foundation of unbelievable compliments, your partner won't want to hear them again, at least not from you, which will kill your dirty talking goals.

Giving your partner false hopes

During dirty talking moments, although you want to please your partner, refuse the urge to give fake promises. Don't bring up fantasies you can never fulfill. For instance, don't say talks like, *"I want to do a threesome with you,"* *"can we try voyeuristic sex?"*, *"I love BDSM"* when you know they are a step over the line for you.

Talking about these fake fantasies will create mental imagery in his mind, and you will be surprised when he will want to fulfill those fantasies. Now imagine what will happen if he finds out you were only fooling him. *Bad, right?* That's more reason to stay away from fake fantasies.

Laughing at your partner's lines

Don't try it. Runaway as far as possible from this mistake because it will most likely end your dirty talking streak.

I know when your lover attempts to dirty talk, it may sound *awkward,* and you may feel the urge to laugh aloud. However, perish the urge; suppress the laugh as quickly as it comes to your mind. Encourage that lover even if the dirty talk used sounds funny; kiss him instead of laughing. Simply put, do something positive and prevent that laughter.

Being repetitive

Have you ever liked a song with one line from beginning to end? Wait! Is there a song with one line from start to finish? I don't think so because I haven't heard one and wouldn't want to because it will eventually be tiring, and I will want to block my ears—likewise repetitive dirty talks.

I know sometimes you will go blank and wouldn't know what word to say. However, it doesn't warrant you to continue repeating a statement or question.

When you lack words, try asking questions. For instance, whenever I'm dirty talking, and I go blank after using statements like, *"fuck me."* I immediately start the question version.

"Oh, God. Do you know I miss your dick?"

"Is my pussy yours? Can you handle the heat?"

With this, I don't have to repeat, *"Oh, fuck me"* throughout. It will kill the sexual tension.

Remember, going blank is expected because no one has a dirty talk dictionary planted in their brain. But, repeating a word, phrase, or statement is a mistake that should be staunchly avoided.

Trying to force it

Human beings aren't created the same way. Hence, everything will not work for everyone. Trying to talk dirty may not work for you at first, maybe because of nervousness or lack of confidence. Hence, you shouldn't force the talk. Let it flow, feel the vibe, and your partner will enjoy the talk. Surprisingly, most times, men know when a woman is forcing the talk. This is a turn-off, and you may end up even killing sexual energy.

Let me give you an advice...

First, I don't believe in success without pain/struggles. So, surely, you will make mistakes, believe me, your mistake might not even be a mistake to you, but it affects your partner adversely, and you get to find out after the deed has been done. But you know the good thing about mistakes? They make you better. So, when you make them, that doesn't mean you should hand the boots of talking dirty because of the slip. Apologize and work to be better and very soon, you would have successfully introduced talking dirty in your bedroom, your partner would be comfortable with it, and I'm damn sure that mistakes won't fuck with you ever again.

SUMMARY

- ✓ Before sex, say what you want during sex, say what you like
- ✓ Gauge his reaction
- ✓ Take charge

Common mistakes in talking dirty

- ✓ Too much profanity
- ✓ Applying dirty talk from porn
- ✓ Talking non-stop
- ✓ Talking unbelievably
- ✓ Giving your partner false hopes
- ✓ Laughing at your partner's lines
- ✓ Being repetitive
- ✓ Trying to force it

Chapter 8: Live the Talk

Skype/video calls

Have you ever tried X-rated video calling, and it went wrong? Do you want to try it out and don't want to fail? Worry and search no more because this chapter contains everything you need to become a maestro in Skype/video sex calls.

I believe most of us aren't new to saying sexy things on the phone. However, we are now in a generation where we can't only talk to loved ones; they can also be seen from anywhere around the globe with a smartphone and laptops. Having a sexy Skype session with your lover builds intimacy, sexual tension and adds the necessary spice to your sex life. But, if your partner isn't close by for that quickie or is far away for a Friday-Sunday showdown, then Skype and video calls are your best bets in making your lover want you badly.

Over the years, I've met clients and friends who tried using Skype or video calls to spice up their sex life. However, only a few enjoyed the spicy sex life for a long time. After a series of questions, I discovered that the rejuvenated sex life doesn't last because the couples aren't naughty or freaky, but because their Skype or video call sessions lacked proper preparations and creativity. Let's face the truth. Following one routine or action for an extended period leads to a decline in want for that action, right? This is why most people later become terrible at it. Imagine that the only thing you do in every Skype session is to stay naked in front of the camera, playing with yourself, and your partner does likewise. What will happen after a month? Will you still drool when you see your partner's body like you did when you saw it on the first day? No! Hence, preparation matters! Creativity is also crucial.

How do you prepare?

Preparing for Skype or video sex calls is relatively easy and requires some little steps.

Treat it like a real date

First, you need to take your Skype session seriously. Treat it like you are going on a date, dress up nicely, wear that sexy lingerie, that fabulous dress, apply your best perfume, and *kill it!* Your Skype session should be top-notch, and it all begins from the way you see it. Prepare the same way you would for a date.

Eliminate every distraction

You must get rid of everything and anything that will cause a break in communication between you and your lover. For instance, imagine that you are on a video call, naked, and the mood between you and your lover is about to blow off the roof. Then, suddenly, someone barges into your room. What will become of you? It's simple! First, you will be distracted, embarrassed (perhaps) and of course, there will be a significant decline in the mood between you and your lover. You and your lover might find it funny and have a good laugh. However, it's most likely going to be the end of the call.

So, in all that you do, before commencing the video call or Skype, cancel out distractions. Do you think your phone will be a significant distraction due to friends who call every time? Put it off or on airplane mode. Do you have a roommate or a relative sharing your home? Get a room with a good lock and lock the door. Also, don't forget to close the blinds.

Do everything possible to eliminate all distractions around you. Turn off that loud music which prevents you from hearing your lover's comments, put your baby to bed if their constant attention- seeking will prevent you from concentrating; give that kid some dollars to go shopping for candy while you have the house to yourself. Make sure your attention on your lover is undivided. This way, your sole concentration would be in creating the mood and making that lover horny, which will lead to wild sexual adventures.

Get erotic before the video/Skype session

This is quite important to the success and longevity of every video call or Skype. The truth is that sex through videos and Skype isn't like the real deal, which is based on physicality. Video chats dwell on imagination, the ability of your lover to think creatively about what he wants to do to you when you meet, and this is what makes it spicy. So, before starting the video, take a long shower, connect bodily. Watch some X-rated movies and read a good erotica book. If possible, engage in self-pleasure some minutes before starting the call.

In short, anything that creates a connection to your body is allowed, anything that makes you horny. This will give you the energy and vibe required for your video, and I bet you, your lover, will take cognizance of it.

Tidy up your surroundings

The final preparation before commencing your Skype sex session or video call is to treat your surroundings just like your body by showering enough love on it.

Skyping in an unkempt room can serve as a distraction to your partner, which will truncate your endeavors in giving your partner that pleasure. Hence, before the start time, spare a couple of minutes to clean up. Pick up that laundry lying carelessly on the floor, make your bed even if you aren't going to use it for your Skype session. If you plan to use a cushion for the session, place it in a perfect place; work with the lights to ensure your partner gets a good view of what you are selling.

This way, your partner doesn't get to see your room untidy and allows your attention to remain undivided, and you won't be thinking about the chores that are piled up for you until you are done with the Skype sex session.

When you have fully prepared yourself for the Skype sex session, it becomes effortless to get your lover in the mood. He will notice your preparations, which will make him excited and equally horny.

However, if your lover isn't responding to the level you want, then you can also introduce these quick tricks.

Reminiscing on a memory together

An excellent way to get your lover in the mood is to be reminiscent of past sexual experiences. Talk about those lovely sexual memories; do away with the fights and quarrels. Talk about those mind-blowing moments. For instance, you can talk about a time when you had sex in the shower, kitchen, etc. Talk about how you liked it. Indeed, he will join you and talk about some sexual moments, and in a couple of minutes, you will be horny, full of sweet memories, and happy.

Being reminiscent is the easiest way to turn up the mood, and it always works! Bring back those memories, let him tell you what you have done that almost ripped him apart with waves upon waves of pleasure, tell him how you plan to do that same action when you meet him. You will see the fire of desire burning in his eyes, and he will be filled with thoughts and imagination, which will turn up the mood.

Dirty talk

Don't tell me you plan to turn up the mood without some good dirty talks. I will be offended!

Engage in some dirty talks even while reminiscing on those memories. Add those moans with a sexy voice, give those compliments, ask those questions, and say those statements without being shy. Here are some cool ideas for you.

"Ooh... You want that?"

"I get turned on when you talk that way."

"You look ravishing."

"I'm getting so wet, babe."

"I'm so wet. I wish you could take a dive, honey."

"Arrrhh...your body looks yummy."

"What do you want me to do to myself?"

"OMG, you are going to make me cum!"

Dirty talks work on the mind and also create an image of you deep in your lover's imagination. It's essential and shouldn't be neglected.

Read something sexy to each other

This is another way to set the mood for the action. Give your partner some time to write after asking him this question, *"are there any sexy things you can say about me?"* Prepare yours without letting him know and tell him once he is done with yours. Simple, right?

Once these tips have been used, then your partner is most likely already in the mood waiting for your freakiness. It's now time for the main thing.

What do you do after creating the mood? How do you sustain the sexual tension? It's simple! Here comes the creativity!

Stay in the frame

While skyping with your lover, it is relatively easy to get carried away, and your partner would begin to strain his eyes to get a good look at you. It's quite terrible if your partner gets to see your face alone, and he is unable to see the priceless assets below. So, when skyping, ensure your camera is at the right angle, which allows your partner that perfect view of your body at all times.

(*An extra tip*) make sure the part of your body that your lover likes the most is appropriately illuminated. For instance, whenever I Skype, I always remember that my lover is a breast man, and I put those babies in full view. Hence, discover that body part that sends him to the moon and display it adequately.

Striptease

You don't have to be a professional stripper to perform a striptease. The only requirement is the mindset of pleasuring your lover. Put on that lovely attitude, attempt to show more but reveal less, and put on that lovely striptease.

Make use of toys and props

Ooooh... This is the icing to the cake, another level of freakiness to boost that sexual tension.

Get some good sex toys and props and advice your partner to get some too. Try that vibrator, try that butt plug, use them as you like, and your lover will anticipate every Skype and video call session.

Finish off with a good sext

An excellent way to finish the Skype or video call is to sext with your partner after the video. Here are some ideas for you.

Jane: *Thanks, babe, for today. I'm horny and wet. Can't wait to see you, baby.*

Simon: *I've done nothing, baby. Thank you too. I'll see you soon. Can't wait to eat you up!*

Let's look at another idea

Jane: *I loved it! Can we meet right now? I miss you.*

Simon: *I know, right... I want it too. I'll see you soon, I promise.*

Sexting while using foreshadowing helps in preserving the tension and creates an image of your next sexual experience with your partner. Follow these tips, and your skype/video chat sex experience will be worthwhile!

So let me wrap this up with this little gift for you. I believe that should be under these three categories

- *I've had video sex before*
- *I have an idea about it, but I've never tried it before*
- *I dislike it but right now, I don't give a fuck about my likes and dislikes, so long as my sex life is on fire and myself and my partner are sexually satisfied.*

Whatever category you may fall into, you should know that video sex/skype is the real deal, a sure way to preserve sexual tension. Once you love and trust your partner, there is no limit to the emotional and sexual benefits you can get from video sex. So, don't be scared and unlock those inner desires.

SUMMARY

- ✓ Treat it like a real date
- ✓ Eliminate every distraction
- ✓ Get erotic before the video/Skype session
- ✓ Tidy up your surroundings
- ✓ Reminiscing on a memory together
- ✓ Dirty talk
- ✓ Read something sexy to each other
- ✓ Stay in the frame
- ✓ Striptease
- ✓ Make use of toys and props
- ✓ Finish off with a good sext

Chapter 9: Live the Talk

Cybersex and phone sex

Once I had a friend who used to engage in cybersex in AOL chats. Therein, she would meet strangers, and she would talk nasty, get turned on, and possibly get off. According to what she told me; it was an explosive experience; she always felt good. Now, technology has taken over, and humans do not have to have to perform cybersex through the exclusive use of text. This is due to the availability of Face Time, video calls, and other platforms. This modern medium of cybersex makes it interesting as you do not only get to use your imagination to determine what the person on the other end of the text is doing you can also see the assets of your lover, which drives you crazy. Among the younger generation, cybersex is the real deal, and it is also helpful in creating the mood and preserving sex life among couples. I mean, who doesn't like to see one's sex partner that isn't with us at the moment? I bet the answer would be nobody.

This chapter covers the secrets of cybersex and essential information to become a veteran in phone sex.

Let's look at cybersex

Cybersex isn't a singular action; instead, it is one that cut across a series of actions with only a similarity; that is, it is done over the internet. It is also known as virtual sex, and it isn't based on physicality. Cybersex can be between a couple or a group.

Cybersex is safe

As conversations and fantasies build over the internet, you are at no risk of contracting any sexually transmitted disease or prone to pregnancy. Although cybersex isn't void of all risk, it is still the most preferred option among unmarried people.

How to have cybersex

Cybersex is easy and safe once the proper rules are followed. Here are tips for enjoying smooth cybersex.

Leave your face out if you are too shy

Are you the type of person that is always shy of your lover seeing your nude? Do you feel inferior, but you desire cybersex? Listen to me!

The first rule and a good one for comfortable cybersex are to leave out the face. It's entirely unwise to add your face to the camera when your cybersex partner seeks to get off by looking at your assets. Place the camera in a position that leaves out the whole face, put on those tinted glasses in your drawer, or wear that favorite mask and fulfill your cybersex fantasies.

Break out with emoji's

While using a chat system, saying everything will be too revealing, don't you think? Leave your partner guessing by breaking out with some cool emoji's, activate that freakiness.

Do you understand emoji? Take a step back to the first chapter and learn how to use them.

Use those cool emoji's, let him think about those raunchy meanings attached to them. This way, you are creating a mood, and your cyber sex will be a success!

Safety precautions

Cybersex aids relationship connections and improves romance among couples. It is a medium that uses video and audio to simulate real-life sex. However, if you want to attempt cyber sex, it's best to be safe, and set boundaries. I believe you don't want to be at an important business meeting and receiving nude photos from that lover, right? Of course, not! Hence, the need to schedule the time you sent sexy messages to your partner.

Hence, to stay safe set those boundaries.

What do you want your lover to say? What words are steps over the line? What sexual acts are ok with you? What actions are forbidden? Set those boundaries to be safe. Make a list of prohibited things, things that don't get you off or turn you on and inform your lover about them.

Don't forget that being safe is the beginning of the mind-blowing sexual experience. Hence, setting those personal limits is compulsory to remain safe.

Common mistakes to avoid in cybersex

Live every date experience; proper planning is essential to avoid any mistakes, likewise virtual sex. Here's a list of common mistakes and tips on how to surmount them.

Not setting boundaries

Before you connect virtually, it's vital to ensure that it is consensual, and all boundaries have been discussed. Create a conversation on the sexual acts that are comfortable to you and the ones you are willing to try. Also, create time for the ones you seek to prevent, the no-go-areas.

Talk about the amount of skin you are going to reveal, what excites you, your fantasies, etc. If it is video sex, talk about if it's okay to take a screenshot or recordings of sessions.

Once discussed, you are less susceptible to make those mistakes, and your lover won't go over the line.

Not using a safe cyber platform

Although cybersex is without complications such as STD or pregnancy, and you aren't required to be on contraceptives, you are still obligated to be safe. Having a good understanding of cybersex before engaging in it helps in reducing the chances of failure and regret.

Even if you trust your partner, there have been cases of partners who broke the trust their lovers had in them by revealing sensitive pictures and videos to others. While this doesn't mean you shouldn't engage in cybersex, it's best to play safe.

Most preferably, use a phone which is up to date rather than a laptop, use any platform which offers end-to-end encryption, and make yourself anonymous by using emails that cannot be linked back to you. Also, make sure you use the right password and, if possible, activate the two-step verification process.

Finally, do you have a birthmark or tattoo known by almost everyone around you? Do you have any mark on your body that allows people to identify you easily? Are you living in a well-known area? Use the element of disguise and make yourself unidentifiable.

Accessing your lover will determine if you should proceed with virtual sex or wait for the physical one. Has your lover made you feel uncomfortable before? During the times spent together, did you feel safe? Once these are answered, you will know if you are safe or otherwise.

Not using the right lights

Most times, we all want our lover to see those sexy body parts clearly, and instead of looking beautiful, we kill the fun because our lighting is poor. Poor here doesn't mean the lighting is too low but too bright.

Try opting for low light, romantic ones that illuminate your body adequately. Also, ensure that the light isn't behind you. It must always be in front of you to give your lover the right view.

***Ending the virtual sex or chat immediately after the
action.***
This mistake is common in almost all women. After the
action and perhaps you both got off, it's important to
show care and attention before dropping the call. If you
are chatting, say a compliment, talk about the experience,
and thank that lover without necessarily saying thank you.

If it's a video, also say some sexy compliment, heap some
praises on that lover, ask if they enjoyed it, and talk about
plans. This will tell your lover that you care and cherish
them.

Finally, cybersex is healthy, safe, and useful once done
correctly. If you seek to engage in it, make sure you don't
make these mistakes.

Phone sex
Now you are a maestro in sexting and cybersex, but you
are still in search of ways to get creative with your lover.
Fortunately, there is always one that sets lovers on fire:
phone sex.

Indeed, I know you must wonder how to go about phone
sex, how to successfully progress from saying dirty talks
in-person to displaying it on phone conversations. Before
these thoughts overwhelm you, I should inform you that
phone sex may seem daunting, but, if done right, you will

be surprised that you may even be hit with waves of orgasms.

Phone sex seems awkward because it is dependent on the intensity of a conversation between two lovers. It is solely dependent on the ability of lovers to be highly descriptive, being able to create that spicy image that promotes arousal in your partner.

How to have phone sex

Having phone sex is comfortable with these steps

Ask for consent

Before you kick start any sexual activity, physically or technologically, it's always best to get consent and equally give consent to your partner. Most preferably, text before the action and ask for permission from your partner. This will be a record for you, and it will make the encounter safer.

Now, when I said consent, I don't mean that you should say, *"Baby, I need your consent before we start."* Don't do that. You aren't a detective. You need to be creative when seeking consent. Here are some ideas.

Recently, you are the subject of my fantasy. Do you have free time when I can tell you all my wild and dirty fantasies through the phone?

I miss it when we fuck. Are you up for some phone sex on Friday night?

Babe, you look so hot. Do you mind if I call and tell you everything that I'm going to do to your body when we meet?

Seeing each other is almost impossible for the next few weeks. It got me thinking about you, and I want to try out some cheesy phone sex with you. Are you game?

If you sense any hesitation from your lover, it's okay to enquire from them the reason why they don't like the idea and check if you can change their mindset. For instance, if your lover isn't comfortable due to the presence of others around him, substitute phone sex for sexting or video sex chat.

Moreover, your partner's interest in phone sex is subject to change. Hence, it is essential to seek consent before commencing any phone sex.

Ask about body preference words

If your relationship isn't a new one, there is a possibility that you already know the words that your partner loves to hear. However, if you are new, it's advised to ask about body preference words. Earlier, we have discussed how to ask for your partner's preference as relating to their body parts. By this, it's not strange to you, right? Of course, it isn't. Does he like cock, dick, penis, stick, or anaconda, does he enjoy when you say tits, boobs, or breasts, does he like ass or butt, cum or sperm. Getting familiar with the words suitable to your lover allows you to pleasure them adequately and ensures that they don't get offended when you say some words.

Familiarize yourself with the language of lust

During the phone sex or before it, you must understand the language of lust. It will help in creating the mood and spicing things up. An excellent way to start is by watching porn. Usually, I do recommend reducing to muting the sounds. However, if you are just like me, who gets turned on by what I hear more than what I see, then using your air pods would work wonderfully. Watch a couple of porn videos. Check out those X-rated scenes in movies and while doing that, think about your lover.

If you aren't into porn, another alternative is picking an erotica book and bury yourself in them. If you find fantasies like BDSM a turn on, read a part of 50 Shades of Grey. Read that favorite erotica and get wet for your lover.

If you cannot get your access to porn videos or erotica, go online and download some erotica audios. Quietly listen while imagining your lover. With this, you will be filled with lust after that lover and will perfectly understand its language.

Set the scene

I know you must wonder why you need to set the scene if it's going to be a phone sex session. However, setting the scene is pivotal to the success of any phone sex.

A couple of years back, I met a phone-sex worker who told me that she usually dressed up sexily and decorated her room with candles before taking calls. I was tempted to ask "why," and she replied, "It makes it look real and puts me in the mood. With it, I'm able to become the woman he's always fantasized about."

I do not need to inform you further on the importance of setting the right scene. Just like it is imperative to prepare for dates, it's also essential to set the scene before any phone sex.

Getting started...

Now, imagine you are in a phone sex session, and you have set the scene, understood the language of lust, and you can build the required sexual tension for mind-blowing phone sex. How do you preserve it? How do you get creative and keep that partner drunk with lust and pleasure? Let's look at some ideas.

Mutually masturbate

One way to keep the sexual tension is to masturbate mutually. There are two ways to initiate this, that is, *Tell or Ask.* Using the *tell* method, you say, *"babe, I want you to listen to me while I'm masturbating."* Then you begin, and from listening to your moans, he will also join you. The *ask* approach is just for you to make a request. You say, *"Love, can we masturbate together"* or *"babe, I want to hear you masturbate."* And you both will begin masturbating, listening to your breath and moans. However, there are other spices you can add to improve your phone sex experience while mutually masturbating rather than just breaths and moans. Let's check out some of them.

Explain what you are doing

Explaining and describing what you are doing is an excellent way to benefit from masturbating. Give in detail how you are pleasuring yourself. Let's look at some examples.

"My fingers are buried deep inside me. It feels good, but your dick is better."

"Smooching my breasts with my fingers makes me wet. Oh, God, my breasts need your lips."

Being descriptive and explanatory allows your lover to imagine you and leads to incredible orgasms.

Reminisce on a memory

If you feel being descriptive isn't doing the magic, try reminiscing on a memory. Talk about a sexual experience; describe it as if your lover was watching. Talk about the way it felt good and hot. It is also good to employ the what-if questions strategy. Check out these examples.

What would happen if I didn't stop wiggling my butt on your dick?

What if I didn't stop sucking you?

Bring back those sexy memories is a way to build the sexual tension on solid grounds.

Explore a fantasy

During phone sex, it is quite safe to explore your fantasies. Talk about ideas like having sex in the pool, in a cinema, in a helicopter, in a public place, BDSM, etc. Talk about those fantasies, especially if you know the ones your lover likes. Use words to make these fantasies look real.

Staying in the moment

While having the phone sex of your dreams, there are times when it can look overwhelming due to happiness and pleasure, and you may be forced to stay silent, laugh/giggle. However, it's okay to be quiet during phone sex. Sometimes, when there is no vibe to say a word during phone sex, I usually ask my partner questions like, "*so, what would you do to me when we meet?*" then I keep quiet and get turned on with his comments. So, it's normal to be silent sometimes.

Don't be scared to laugh or giggle with your lover. Laughing and giggling is bound to happen in every phone sex session because it is a good sign that you guys are comfortable. Let out that loud laugh when your lover does something funny. Let him laugh a couple of times too. This doesn't mean the sexual tension will decrease. See laughter as a sexual break before another wave of freakiness.

It is always best to remain true to yourself during the session. Enjoy the fun, and don't be a tool to your lover. It's a medium to ensure you and your lover both have fun. So, be true to yourself, do what only you will do.

I've met a couple of women who want to engage in phone sex but find it awkward, which hindered them from doing it. Thus, I wondered, how can we rid ourselves of awkwardness in phone sex?

Let's take a quick lesson from phone-sex operators.

Phone sex operators are never awkward, and it made me wonder how they go about it. After a couple of readings, I found out a secret.

The first step every phone sex worker does is to classify the caller. Is he/she shy, sophisticated, borderline nasty, or sultry? And you should do the same. Since you have spent some time with your lover, you should know the class the person falls under. Once classified, it becomes easy to tell the shy guy to listen when you masturbate and put him in the mood which removes awkwardness, or to paint a fantasy for the sultry which creates the hot conversation and removes awkwardness, or to mutually masturbate with the sophisticated or to ask the borderline nasty caller what he wants to do to her. These ways are used to remove the awkwardness, and you can do the same.

Another way to remove awkwardness is to play a porn video, most preferably in the background. Increase the volume to the right level where your lover can hear, and it won't be unpleasant by preventing easy communication between you and your lover. This will probably lead to a question from your partner and a laugh from you too. Then, you can start the questions attack, and there will be no awkward moments between you and your lover.

Common mistakes to avoid

Not setting boundaries

In everything you do, ensure that you set the limits. Let your lover know the words, requests, and phrases that are in the red zone and communicate them well.

Lacking understanding of your lover's body preferences

This will kill sexual tension and destroy the chances of successful phone sex. Know what your lover likes. Is he the shy type that hates nasty words? Is he cool with all dirty words, or is he selective? Know all this information before you start to talk!

Finally, if you seek to engage in cybersex or phone sex, you should do two things. Stay comfortable and enjoy the action. Cybersex is fun. Phone sex is fun. Introduce your partner to these secrets, and you will be surprised at the level of sexual tension and mind-blowing sex you will reap.

Brianna is a decent woman who wants to engage in phone sex or cybersex, but she Is reluctant because of her culture. This configuration taught that engaging in anything other than physical sex simply means she is selling herself cheap, reducing her worth in the eyes of her lover. Do you believe in such an ideology? Who told you so? Let me blow your mind...if your partner loves you and desires you, using cyber sex or phone sex will only make it better! So, don't be scared of your invisible worth reducing and enjoy the beauties of phone sex and cybersex.

SUMMARY

Cybersex is safe

- ✓ Leave your face out if you are too shy
- ✓ Break out with emoji's
- ✓ Set those boundaries.

How to have phone sex

- ✓ Ask for consent
- ✓ Ask about body preference words
- ✓ Familiarize yourself with the language of lust
- ✓ Set the scene
- ✓ Mutually masturbate
- ✓ Explain what you are doing
- ✓ Reminisce on a memory
- ✓ Explore a fantasy
- ✓ Staying in the moment

Chapter 10: Live the Talk

Role Play

Are you interested in role play? This is a chapter just for you!

Role-playing affords you the chance to get involved in a sexual game where you and your lover take up different characters. It is a medium to let out your naughty side, and it is done using acting, dressing up as a character, which is most times the subject of one's fantasy.

A good reason why role play is good for lovers is that it aids you to surmount your inhibitions. You can try out things you would typically not do. It allows you to control your inhibitions.

Sadly, most people don't buy into the idea of role-playing because they want to avoid feeling embarrassed when suggesting it to their partner. They don't want their fantasies to be used as a yardstick in judging their personalities, or they are scared of not being good in acting out the role. However, role-playing isn't hard, and it's relatively easy to do using these tips.

Start by easing him into It

Every sexual experience requires one party to ease the other into it, and the easiest way to pull this off is by talking. I bet you don't want to scare the shit out of your lover by entering the bedroom dressed as a doctor in full operational gear. So, talk to him about it. While you can take the bull by its horns and say, *"Babe, I want to role-play. What do you think?"* you can quickly start the talk when you notice a role-play scenario when you are with your lover. For example, when I see a pizza delivery guy, I say to my man, *"a pizza delivery outfit is hot. Babe, you will look smashing in an outfit like that. I will kill for delivery from you."* Or you could search for some cool role play costumes online and ask what he thinks about it.

Find a scenario

Since you came up with the idea, you should have a scenario in your bank just in case he asks what you have in mind. Think about your fantasy and create something sexy. When he asks for an idea, you could say, *"last night, I had a sexy dream which made me touch myself. You were royalty, and I was your servant. Always at your command. I will love that."* Wow! The scenario is successfully communicated. If he isn't comfortable, you will be surprised that he might have something wilder and sexier in his arsenal. So, prepare your scenario.

Tell him it's one of your fantasies and you would like to try it with him

Another way to ensure that your role play introduction is successful is to inform your man that it's one of your fantasies. For a record, men tend to meet the needs of their women, especially if they love you. So, you have a 99% success rate that he would want to try it out. If he knows all your fantasies, then your scenario must match that of your fantasies.

Make the bedroom free of all judgments

To achieve mind-blowing sex from role-playing, each partner must be open-minded, free to discuss numerous fantasies and wants without fear of disapproval. Hence, before you start the role play, give your partner your word, and they should follow suit that laughing at actions, fantasies, and acting performances won't happen during the act. If you are both going to laugh about the role play, after it has been completed, it must be healthy and not a chance to mock another partner. Also, note that role-playing is a private act between lovers and shouldn't be a discussion with third parties even if the person is a relative. The sexual act is a point of vulnerability for all humans. Hence, it's best to assure and be assured that you won't be judged by your lover for maximum success and longevity.

Fantasies aren't always similar to lifestyle

Our preference in our sex life often differs from our lifestyle. Since I started to read and write to this day, I've heard numerous role play fantasies, and they are most times unrelated to the actor's lifestyle. A staunch advocate of feminism who loves to be dominated in bed, a nurse who loves to be a slave, a contractor who would kill to be a stripper, etc.

Most times, people are faced with the difficulty of accepting their sexual wants because they are significantly different from their daily lives. However, role-playing isn't about lifestyle; instead, it is based on pleasure, contentment and uniting both personalities is the key to success. Once the act is consensual, there should be no limit to sex life.

Begin with words

I wouldn't advise you to start role-playing by dressing like a slave while he dresses as a Roman Praetorian. It will most likely be uncomfortable and overwhelming. Hence, begin with words while taking that missionary position. For instance, if you are acting out the police officer/shoplifter play, you could say, *"I'm sorry. I know I'm a bad girl for taking those candies. Please let me go. I will do anything. Please, my mum will kill me if she finds out."* Make use of words and create imagery of what you will do when there is a costume. Once comfortable with the words, then you can spice things up with some outfits.

Set your limits before engaging in the act

With role-playing, it's possible to say and do things that you will not engage in elsewhere. So, set a limit with your lover. You may have given consent to a scenario. But you cannot envisage the direction where it will lead. Hence, your limitations are necessary. Also, it is possible to give consent to a role play, and you won't be feeling the vibe when acting it out. This is why it is always advised to have a safe word. Remember, set limits before the act.

Choose from a list

If you aren't sure of the scenario to use, it can become discouraging. However, I should inform you that it isn't your responsibility always to bring the scenario for role-playing. To ease you into role-playing, here is a list of a possible scenario. I don't mind if you make this your list. You can consider it a gift.

- Strangers in a pub
- Erotic massager and client
- Teacher and student
- King and slave
- Boss and maid
- Doctor and patient
- Work supervisor and intern
- Boss and secretary
- A police officer and criminal
- Rock star and diehard fan
- Football captain and cheerleader

Let's explore some scenarios

Spicy delivery

Are you tired of cooking? This is for you. Here is your scenario. You ordered a chicken pepperoni pizza, and when the hot delivery guy arrives, you realize you have no money. Then you ask if you can pay using another platform... I know you have got the idea.

Hypnotized

Do you want to get over those inhibitions? Check this out.

You are hypnotized, and your man is the hypnotist. You are under his control, and he is going to do whatever he wants to you.

Please officer

You ran a light and got pulled over. Then you discovered that the cop is hot, and you would do anything to make him overlook your offense.

My parents are in the other room

You are studying in your room with a tutor who is freaking hot, and you switch on the seduction mode. Your goal is to get laid.

There are lots of scenarios, and you just need to search on the internet for some ideas.

Here are common mistakes to avoid when you attempt role playing

Improvisation

When your role play isn't properly scripted, then you are most likely going to try a bit of improvising, which will make your situation awkward. When you don't have an idea of what to say, most times, you end up saying something wrong. So, get a script and enjoy the play.

Forcing it

One good thing about role-playing is that a thousand people can play one character in a thousand ways. So, don't try too hard. Don't force it. Use a method that works for you!

Going too far

It's relatively easy to go overboard when role-playing. There will be a time when you will bite too hard or spank badly, and this won't go down well with your lover. Also, you may even say some words that are not acceptable by your lover. So, know your partner, drop those nasty words and avoid going too far.

Role-playing is an adventure for you and your lover. So, don't limit yourself. Explore your lover's fantasies as well as yours, and you will see that it's worth it.

There is this woman I read about some years ago. She was always busy with work, and her sex and marital life were in shambles. When she realized this, she was shoulder deep into her work, and her husband was almost out of the equation. She needs her husband to want her again, and she knew spreading those legs won't do the required trick. Then, role-playing came knocking. She left her work earlier than usual, got a French maid kit from the sex store, and rushed home. After taking time making everywhere neat and smooth, she dressed up for her man. When he got back, of course, he was stunned and horny. All buried hormones let loose, and it was indeed a sexual adventure. Role-playing is a tool that is inevitable for every woman. Do you have it in your sexual toolbox?

SUMMARY

Roleplaying

- ✓ Start By Easing Him into It
- ✓ Find a Scenario
- ✓ Tell Him It's One of Your Fantasies and You Would Like To Try It with Him
- ✓ Make the Bedroom Free Of All Judgments
- ✓ Fantasies Aren't Always Similar To Lifestyle
- ✓ Begin With Words
- ✓ Set your limits

Chapter 11: Practice

The Dirty Talk

Now you have learned the psychology behind the dirty talk, ways to introduce it to your lover, other ways to use dirty talk in cyber and phone sex, and tips to enjoy role-playing, it's now time to practice dirty talking.

Exercise 1: building a list of words and phrases that you like

Now you know what dirty talk means and also have an idea of dirty talks. It has now reached the stage to create your list of dirty words and phrases. Call it your dirty talk dictionary; this is where you can refer to when you are bereft of dirty words or phrases to use.

Create a list of parts of speech in dirty talks: dirty talk nouns, and adjectives. Put in the words you know are comfortable with your lover and the words you like.

If you are pretty stumped on what to do, check the next chapter for dirty talks and use them as a jump start.

Exercise 2: create an off-limits of words or phrases you don't like

Off-limits are as crucial as your dirty talk dictionary. Choose those words that are body-shaming or mood deteriorating, whatever makes you feel awful.

The best way to know words you dislike is to pick out the words you like. What body parts turn you on? What body part doesn't affect you? What body parts don't you want to talk about? This way, you can quickly get the off-limits. If possible, ask your partner for his off-limits instead of trying to figure it out.

Remember, there are some off-limits you may find out during sex. So, be prepared. Never say utter negative replies to dirty talk. Try to offer alternatives that get you off and let him have a peek at your dictionary if possible.

Exercise 3: gradually working your way up to talking dirty

Once you have completed exercises 1 and 2, it's now time to talk about the talk. This is where you bring your partner into the picture. Remember that your partner might also want to develop dirty talking by creating his list of words, so be open-minded.

Once your partner understands what dirty talk means, you can gradually start talking, perhaps using virtual sex or phone sex sessions, or sexting. If you have sex regularly, **start with a good moan**, then move to say **"ooh", "yeah", "hmm", afterward**, move to **"oh, yes! Give it to me"** - before going to the real deal.

Pay keen attention to your words, its effect on your lover, his words, if there are adoptable, and try adding them to your dictionary.

Exercise 4: practice your sounds and whispers
It is one thing to talk dirty, and another one to do it with the right sounds and using the power of whispers to your advantage.

Increase the moans during sex; do it sexily. Use your sexy voice when you dirty talk. Whisper that sexy comments in front of a mirror, try it on your lover in public. With this, you will understand the power of sound and whispers.

Exercise 5: stay true to yourself
This is an essential exercise to be a successful dirty talker. You mustn't fake it. Staying true to yourself emits an unmatched vibe. Men tend to know when a woman is

faking it. It's like a natural skill. Hence, if you want to create the mood successfully, stay true to yourself.

Ask yourself, *"what do I love doing?" "What am I not comfortable with?"* Make a list of these things and follow them strictly. Do not do something you aren't pleased with. Use the comfortable list at all times.

Exercise 6: rehearse and record

After making a list of your dirty talks and that of your lover, and you have found the sexy voice, the power of whispers, and you can also use sounds to your advantage, then it's time to find out how good you are as a dirty talker.

The test is simple: does your dirty talk sound appealing to you?

Face a mirror, use it as your partner, and get a recorder. Record your dirty talk, try some whispers, and apply sounds. Do this a couple of times and play each session carefully. Did you enjoy it? Did it sound good or goooooood? If it sounds good, rehearse again to make it better. If it doesn't, still rehearse over and over again until you become a maestro at it.

Exercise 7: codify your sex talk

Once you have rehearsed, I bet you should be good at talking dirty, and you need to codify your talk. Once again, ask yourself, *"am I an easy dirty talker", "sultry",* or *"borderline nasty"*. "Is my talk based on a specific fantasy?" Or *"sex in general?"* This will allow you to arrange your talk and also enables easy application.

Exercise 8: talking dirty for fun

I should congratulate you once you reach this stage because you are a step from becoming a badass dirty talker. This last step is talking dirty for fun.

Like I've emphasized throughout the book, dirty talking isn't a bedroom-only activity. To attain the Masters in dirty talk certificate, it's time to talk for fun. Talk while at work to your lover, while on the dining table, in a dinner, when on a date, everywhere! Make dirty talking a daily activity.

I would say clap for yourself, but it's going to be childish. So, congratulations on your success as a dirty talker! I hope your journey is blissful and full of orgasms. The next chapter contains 369 gifts for you! Hurry up and open them!

Chapter 12: Talk the Talk

369 Dirty Talk Examples

Do you want to drive your man crazy with mind-melting and cock-stiffening dirty talks? This chapter will help you press your man's pleasure button and turn him on with saucy dirty lines. Just like sex, dirty talk has to be calibrated to suit your man because what you presume to be dirty may sound weird, offensive, or silly to your man. Remember, dirty talk appeals differently to everyone.

Talking dirty with your man could sometimes feel like walking through an unknown minefield. Most women feel embarrassed and ludicrous at the thought of talking dirty. This could be because they don't know the guidelines or they do, but they simply don't know what to say. The good news is that dirty talks can be learned. This chapter will help boost your confidence in trying out dirty talks if you are the shy type.

Dirty talk is a powerful element of eroticism that is always overlooked. Not only does it charge sexual polarity, but it also creates a steamy aura that improves sex life by activating the power of imagination. Dirty talk is an easy way of enhancing and adding spice to your sex life.

To help you improve your sex life, here are 369 dirty talk examples that would drive your man wild and knock his socks off in bed. I assure you; these examples aren't mere thoughts of subjective experience; they are very accurate and result-oriented. Although the foolproof examples below have been known to work effectively, you have to get the delivery right. *Talk the talk* like you mean it. You can customize each example to best suit you and your man. Enough of the talk, let's get on with the examples, shall we?

Examples of dirty talks to build sexual tension

You must spice up your sexual life by creating an aura of pleasurable sex even before the main action. Use dirty talks to raise the excitement and anticipation of your man-days or weeks to your next rendezvous. If this is done correctly, you would have successfully expressed your sexual energy to turn on your man. In building anticipation for the next sexual experience, use dirty talks to talk about past sexual encounters, sexy things you would like to do to your man, or repeat in your future sex. Some examples of such dirty talks are outlined below. Remember, you can customize each example to suit you and spice things up.

1. Would you fuck me hard tonight like you did last night?

2. Remember how you sucked my pussy so well last night? I want you to do the same tonight, baby.

3. I'm lying on my back staring at my ceiling, wishing I had you on top of me instead.

4. I'm watching this naughty movie online; wish we could see it together.

5. Do you have an idea how badly I want your hard cock filling my cunt with hot cum?

6. Can't get thoughts of last night's romp out of my head; perhaps we should try it again tonight.

7. Would you go down on me right now if I asked you to do so? (Could be used to build sexual tension).

8. I want to fuck you, even though you're not in a good mood.

9. I wish we could have sex all day long (could be used to keep the sexual tension high when he is leaving).

10. You have such a gorgeous cock; It fits into me perfectly.

11. I can't wait to wrap my lips around your throbbing cock.

12. Baby, I'm all yours tonight. Anal or oral?

13. Licking a sweet stick right now and wishing I was licking your cum off your rock-hard cock.

14. I'm yearning to find out if you're as good in reality as you are in my naughty fantasies.

15. Your badass is driving me insane! I want you on my bed.

16. If I place my eyes on you, I'll jerk you off so hard until I get every last drop of cum out of you.

17. My pussy misses your touch and awaits you.

18. I want you to fuck me hard in the bath.

19. I've been very naughty today, and I probably deserve some spanking. Would your cock correct me?

20. I'd rather be riding your sexy dick right now than be at work.

21. I hope your day was as lovely as my sexy ass.

22. I might sound greedy, but I feel like draining your balls tonight.

23. You're the best baby; nobody has ever fucked me so good like you do.

24. Would you prefer I wear panties tonight or thong or nothing?

25. If I weren't at work, I would be on my knees sucking your cock.

26. I'm all yours tonight, baby; I would make you cum so hard.

27. Can't seem to concentrate at work; all I think about is having your throbbing cock inside my wet cunt/pussy. (This is perfect as a message when you are at work).

28. I get helplessly wet when you look at me like that.

29.   You make me feel so horny and wet, baby.

30.   I really can't wait to feel your soft lips on my pussy.

31.   Can't wait to get over with work today; I want to wrap my wet pussy/cunt around your dick/cock.

32.   I want you to make me cum hard tonight, baby.

33.   I get damn wet when you thrust your cock inside me.

34.   Is my pussy yours? Take it!

35.   I feel over the moon when you grind your cock against my ass cheek...

36.   I have a mystery for you to solve, but you'll have to be a special guest tonight between my legs if you're to demystify it.

37.   I've got all the weekend to myself; I could be as loud as you wish, and I intend riding your hard cock all through.

38.   Let's be frank. When next we meet, I'm going to fuck you so hard till you cum in my wet pussy.

39.   Just imagining how it would feel like to have your hard cock stretching my wet pussy right now.

40.   Do you know what I love most about your hard dick?

41.   Baby, I crave for you so much that I feel like sliding off my panties once I set my eyes on you.

42.   Even though we are miles apart, I can perfectly imagine you sliding your hard cock in between my thighs.

43.   The mere sight of your swollen dick makes my pussy quiver.

44.   The magical finger you use on my nipple makes me want you so bad. I'm craving to have your tongue on my hard nipples.

45.   I'm horny, baby, get your irresistible self here.

46.   How you fuck me excites my body. I need to make those hot sounds under your dick.

47.   Your pink lips and smile turn me on. I want to kiss you so desperately.

48.   I really can't wait for you to come to me. Your absence makes me touch myself, and I can't still quench the thirst.

49.   Let's play the sex game. I hope you had enough strength piled up because I am killing you tonight and pretty sure you can't win.

50. Your charming eyes lusting at my burst in that manner makes me horny.

51. Damn, I'm horny! I need the first aid between my thighs.

52. The way you play with my cunt/pussy fills me with intense pleasure.

53. I need you like right now. I'm horny, and my body craves your touch and can't wait.

54. I feel your touch on my chest; keep moving your fingers down. Yea, baby, right there at my pussy, suck me up.

55. Guess what I'm thinking about now... I'm thinking about you and me naked in the shower, and you are banging me so hard from behind.

56. Baby, have you seen a naked woman without a towel lying on the bed, with her legs stretched out and nipples pointing towards you? You should run home.

57. I want to do something nasty like feasting on your cock.

58. I'm sure that no one would know if you put your hand into my pants right now.

59. Can I use my pussy to play on your dick?

60. I'm desperate, why can't we do it right now? I'm pretty sure that none of them will know.

61. Caressing your ass and sucking your dick is better than any lollipop.

62. I want to feel your cum all over my pussy, and my bed soaked in it.

63. I need to feel you inside of me tonight.

64. Relax, let me handle you to a long pleasure blowjob.

65. I need something huge to break me inside; I'm so fucking horny.

66. I want to catch fun tonight. Can you make it happen?

67. All I can imagine is being on the bed right now and having all of you on me immediately.

68. Trust me, I'm going to leave you with no other choice tonight but to shout and scream for a long-lasting erection.

69. Please can you stop looking at me, I mean stop looking at me that way, I'm getting wet already.

70. You are lucky we are at a party, and there are a lot of persons around; I would have jumped on you right away and ensure I get every drop of it.

71. I know this sounds so crazy, but I need to feel your cock in me.

72. I need a penetration right now; can you make it a reality for me.

73. I just thought of doing so many things to you, and I need you in bed right now to accomplish all of it.

74. Just looking straight into your eyes makes me beg for an immediate pussy vibration.

75. I know it might sound greedy, but I want to drill your pussy non-stop tonight. This time, you are not allowed to cum until I tell you to do so.

76. It's so hard to always shut me up with a hot and long kiss.

77. I can't carry on with my work; I find it so hard to settle my mind. All I can think of is you grabbing me, ripping me off my clothes, and fucking the hell out of my cunt.

78. I want you to take control of my body. Put more concentration on my hard nipples and my wet pussy.

79. Hearing your voice gets me all wet for you...Don't let me wait for long.

80. I have no panties under my skirts, and I'm touching myself thinking of you tearing me apart with your hard dick.

81. I'm obsessed with you, and I want you to slowly but steadily, kiss my lips, go down my neck, caress my nipples, suck my nipples, finger me deeply, suck my tits and go all the way down my body fastening your cock into my cunt.

82. I want you staring into my eyes while you fuck me deep.

83. I wish I could have your tasty load of cum in my mouth now.

84. Can't wait to have my face covered with your load of cum.

85. I want to ride your hard-big cock until you fill me with your juice.

86. I feel so good when you're deep inside me.

87. I love the sight of your cock seeking freedom from your pants.

88. Do you know how hot my cunt is right now? It's so wet and ready for your erection.

89. You look so sexy, baby; I want to have you, ride your cock, fuck you, and feel your tongue wandering around my clit.

90. Spank my ass till I'm into it, rough handle my pussy until I get wet and beg you to fuck.

91. I want you to kiss every part of my body, starting from my neck then my lips. Make sure you touch every inch of me.

92. I desire someone to fucking mess me up tonight, and I wish that person could be you.

93. Permit me to handle that...I mean your cock until you lose every vitamin-packed up there.

94. Please make me fucking squirt all over you tonight.

95. No, it's not the rain. I'm wet because I can feel you so close to me. I can't wait for us to get home.

96. I'm going to make you beg before you cum while I orgasm intensely all over you.

97.   I want you to fuck me as hard as you can tonight, roughly handle me until my disturbed cunt begins to jerk.

98.   Oh my god, take over me, fucking ride me harder tonight.

99.   Make me your whore tonight, make me enjoy every bit of pleasure I've missed while you were gone.

100. Yeah, fuck my pussy, daddy, fuck me to my face, fuck me so hard till you ruin my pussy.

101. Oh, fucking destroy my pussy tonight, make it so hard and deep that I begin to sense a need for crutches to walk.

102. Having sex with you is the best feeling I've ever had.

103. I can't take my mind off last night. I want you on me right now; I'm masturbating in the shower.

104. Sex matters are getting out of hand tonight; I need you on the bed right now.

105. I'm wet; all I can think of is you breaking my pussy too hard.

106. I love that...I mean the way you touched me right now.

107. Can you give me a long-lasting pleasure...pussy stimulation? Please do that with something bigger than your finger; you know what I'm talking about, daddy.

108. I need you a little closer to me tonight.

109. I just need hot sex tonight.

110. Tell me how good you feel when you are relaxed, and I'm on top doing the fucking.

111. You have such a nice cock that fits perfectly in my pussy; I would love to taste it one more time.

112. Sure, you will love to taste my juicy pussy.

113. I want a long-lasting fuck, but I need you to tease me, so I beg for it with a wet pussy.

114. If you don't take off your clothes, then you leave me with no other choice but to tear them off cause I'm into it already; I need you on me like now.

115. I couldn't settle my mind on any other thing throughout the day. All I could see is what I will do to you tonight.

116. Make me cum tonight before you do.

117.   I desire to have multiple orgasms tonight; please make it come true.

118.   I wish we were in bed right now; I would ride your cock all night.

119.   Your cock drives me crazy!

Examples of dirty talks during sex

This stage in your sexual experience is fun-filled, and the effect of dirty talks is powerful. When you are in the middle of steamy hot sex, you tend to express how dirty and erotic you are. During sex, you'll notice your mind is free, and you utter more dirty lines. Chances are, you would surprise yourself and say naughty things you never thought of, which is good. Let loose, get nasty, and drive your man wild. You can supercharge the aura around you and your man when you are both naked, making use of some dirty talks outlined below.

120.   I enjoy it when you fuck me like your whore.

121.   Cum all over my sweet wet pussy/cunt.

122.   I love your throbbing hard cock.

123.   Keep diving that nice cock into me just like that; I love it.

124.   Squeeze my breast baby and suck those titties hard.

125. Oh yes, baby, fuck me like you own my pussy.

126. I want to have a taste of my slimy wet cunt from your cock.

127. We aren't done until you fill my mouth with your tasty cum.

128. Fuck me so hard that I can't walk tomorrow.

129. Tell me where you would like to cum after our date tonight.

130. You look sexy tonight.

131. I need you to do an excellent job for me...Somewhere between my legs.

132. I want you to handle me as a sex toy tonight.

133. Oh my god, use me.

134. I fucking need an unstable movement in my pussy.

135. I hope you are ready for me tonight?

136. I will make you cum within seconds.

137. Softly tap my clit till I get wet for a die-hard ride.

138. Your cum feels so good in me that I let out moans of sheer sexual ecstasy.

139. I can't take it anymore, baby, please I want you inside of me now.

140. Yes, baby, dive into me from behind like I'm your slutty whore.

141. Take it, easy baby, I want to relish every inch of your hard cock stretching my wet   pussy.

142. Squeeze my ass just like that baby; it's all yours.

143. I need you on the bed to fucking stimulate this clit of mine.

144. Just make me feel my tight pussy on that huge cock. Take it down tonight.

145. Tell me what you will do to me if you find out I'm already wet?

146. Tell me how hard you can fuck me tonight?

147. Can you drill my pussy till I beg to be released from your huge cock?

148. Tell me how good you feel when I'm on you, riding you so hard till you fill me with the last drop of your delicious cum.

149. You've got such a huge cock; I think we can make good use of it tonight.

150. Can you make tonight one I will always remember?

151. You look very sexy when you orgasm.

152. Does the scent of my pussy juice intoxicate you for a long hard fuck?

153. I want to hear that sound you make when you cum inside of me.

154. Fuck me so hard till I feel my tight pussy clench around your cock.

155. Handle me tonight, so I scream until the neighbors wake up.

156. Tell me what turns you on during a date, I'm fucking horny.

157. I will love it if we could catch fun tonight, though my panties are off.

158. I fucking need a pussy play.

159. I'd love it if you could come over tonight so we can make the sexy dream I had last night a reality.

160. Yeah, baby. I want to taste every drop of your cum in my mouth.

161. Damn! Baby. Please don't stop; I'm cuming.

162. Keep sucking my wet pussy; you're going to make me cum.

163. My pussy is yours. Fuck me; however, you want, baby.

164. Fuck my pussy and fill me with your cum.

165. I love it when you shoot your load inside me.

166. Oh yeah! Fuck me hard, baby.

167. Oh yes! Baby, please continue. I feel so wet when you touch me down there.

168. Oh, yes, baby! I love it when you caress my boobs and pull on my titties.

169. I think it's time we try... (Doggy, cowgirl, reverse cowgirl, anal, etc.).

170. Mmm.... I want you to cum inside me, baby.

171. Please fuck me harder and deeper, baby (pull him towards you as you say this).

172. Use me non-stop like your sex bitch.

173. I love the ride. Keep rocking and riding me... I'm so wet right now; I'm about to cum - please don't stop.

174. I want your dick inside me and feel how wet my pussy is for you.

175. I love the way you arouse me with your fingers. Please, can you make the penetration   deeper.

176. Baby, the way you handling, massaging and caressing my butt and nipple makes me crave for more.

177. Sit back and relax while I take in every inch of you in my mouth.

178. Oh yes! Baby, don't stop. Keep fucking me like that -- Do you like how my pussy   feel?

179. Stroke my clit with your nice hard cock.

180. Oh yes! Baby, this is why I cum always. I love you between my legs.

181. I want to lick every bit of cum out of you.

182. Oh! Yes, baby. Give it to me harder and faster.

183. I love you. Your sweet juicy sexy dick is my perfect meal.

184. I love the way you ride; it makes it hotter and steady. Don't break, please, yea, that's   it, I love it.

185. Keep fucking me, baby, spank my naughty ass harder!

186. I want you to fuck me on top of the kitchen counter!

187. I liked it when you pressed me hard against the bed and applied the pressure down there, fucking me wildly. I can still feel the sensations of your dick inside me.

188. You're so bad, baby. Look at you...

189. I want you to pin me up against the wall and fuck me so hard like it's going to be your last ever. That's it, baby, harder, deeper, I love it.

190. I'm going to make you cum, baby!

191. Do you love how I fuck you, baby?

192. I love feeling the tip of your tongue on my pussy.

193. Baby, make me wet with all your juices. I love it.

194. I love this position; the way you bang me makes me lose count of time.

195. Come on, rip off my panties and fuck me like your little bitch.

196. I love your energy on the bed. Take it in, no going out.

197. You're in control, baby; I want to have my nipples in your mouth.

198. Choke me, baby, raise my legs, spank my fucking ass, I love it.

199. I love how horny you are.

200. Pour your load all over my face. I love feeling you cum all over my face.

201. I love the tits stimulation in this position. It's so hot and sweet.

202. I love the way you are rocking your cock on my sweet pussy.

203. Do it to me the way you like, any manner and form you choose, I'm all yours.

204. Tighten the pinches on the nipple, and yes, suck on them. It drives me crazy.

205. Fuck me while standing; it stimulates me so much.

206. I want you deep inside me, yea, deeper and deeper.

207. I like the sound my breast makes as they applaud when you fuck me like your little bitch.

208. I've been a bad girl, and I think I am enjoying my punishment. Sir, bang me harder.

209. It turns me on every time you pull me close to you. The contact with your stick increases my sexual tension.

210. The sight of your dick makes me horny.

211. Stop talking, and just fuck me!

212. Please, don't ever stop! I love it! You feel so good... Every inch of you...

213. The way you look at me when banging me so hard throws me off balance.

214. Have been seduced by your body, Can I be your sex toy tonight?

215. I want to take these shorts off and give you the best oral sex ever, and I want to do it now!

216. Just feeling your eyes on me makes me so wet.

217. Make me your sex slave. Tie me up, kiss me, press me, fuck me, finger me, kiss me, do to me whatever

you want, whenever you want, anywhere you want, just make me cum.

218. Yes, I love it! Fuck me more! Please, don't ever stop!

219. You turn me on so much.

220. Just get on your knees, and let me show you what I got.

221. Grab my tits, and suck them while I cum.

222. I love it when you're getting so naughty and hot. My baby!

223. Your cock perfectly fits in my pussy. Damn it, fuck me harder!

224. I want you to tie me up and have your way with me.

225. I want you to taste me.

226. Is this pussy yours? Are you going to take it all in?

227. Spread these lips, and fuck me from behind, baby! I love it when you spread my   pussy and fuck me!

228. You look so fucking hot right now.

229. Keep touching me right there. I feel so good right now. Don't stop; please it's making me so wet.

230. I can't get enough of you. I love your cock.

231. Will you be busy tonight? I can't stop craving your cock in my mouth right now.

232. Oh yeah, I can't wait a moment to get down on you once more on my kitchen   counter.

233. I'm daydreaming a long ride with you on my bed and can't get my mind off it.

234. The way you look at me when you are horny is so hot.

235. Tonight, I want you to take advantage of every inch of my body. I want you to fuck me until I forget my name.

236. Baby, what do you want me to do to you?

237. Oh! Turn me over; I love it when you fuck my ass.

238. You like it when I ride you on top, don't you?

239. I can't stop thinking about sitting your face!

240. I fucking love it when you fuck me like a little dirty slut!

241. Please, don't stop being so delicious because I'm all yours.

242. Grab my ass, baby...feeling you all over me already.

243. I just want you to slide your cock between my boobs.

244. Fuck me harder tonight, pull my hair and spank my ass.

245. Show me how hard you can be.

246. Tell me how fast you want me to ride on you.

247. Baby, I want to eat you up completely

248. I am so horny for you; I can't stand it.

249. I've missed the way you kiss me down there, how you hold onto my lips, and how fast you go down on me with that tongue.

250. You're so hard, baby. Tease me with your cock. Let it sit on my pussy and tease it nice and slow... Up and Down....

251. Why do you drive me so crazy?

252. Make me cum for all the nights I haven't for some hours, and it's making me restless.

253. Oh my god, I need you to take over me right now; my body longs for you and you alone. Just make me squirt for you a million times.

254. Just give it to me right away; I need your cock in me. I'm going crazy already.

255. Baby, stop that, you know I need you more than anything. Now, fuck the hell out of   me.

256. I want you now; pull my hair because I need you now. More of that...More!!!!!

257. Make me the dirtiest girl you have known, use me, and get the most amazing sex of your life from me.

258. I just need you to make me suffer in bed; bend me over daddy because I've been a naughty girl.

259. I want you to punish me, spank my ass for being a bad girl.

260. Do me in a way that will stick in my memory forever.

261. This is unbelievable, I'm fucking wet.

262. You make me so horny, I'm playing with my pussy for you.

263. I will never let go of you tonight until you beat that pussy of mine and make it yours.

264. You make me fucking horny; you are the biggest turn on.

265. I'm in love with your body; you owe me tonight.

266. Yeah, baby, you know I go fucking crazy when you talk with me like that, I wished you were right on the bed with me now...I would have done so many things to you.

267. Your cock is huge.

268. I get so wet thinking about you. Do you like how wet my pussy is for you?

269. This pussy is yours, whenever you want it.

270. My nipple is right here; it awaits your touch. Hold it, caress it, suck it, do whatever you want with me. That's it, I love it, harder, harder, you know exactly how I love it, fuck!

271. Baby, I can't stop craving for you inside me. I want you to lick my clits and tits.

272. I love it when you pour the chilled ice-cream on my pussy and suck my tits. It's insane.

273. How do you want me to fuck you? Like this?

274. Pound my wet pussy with your hard cock baby.

275. Baby, I want to feel your hands all over my body.

276. I love it when you fuck my pussy hard like that.

277. Spank my ass baby; I've been a naughty girl.

278. You look so sexy right now.

279. Oh yeah! Wreak my pussy with that fat throbbing cock.

280. I want you to slide your fingers in there, baby...

281. I want you to tie me up, blindfold me, and fuck me any way you'd like.

282. I want to take the full length of your cock in my mouth.

283. Mmmmm... Your cock tastes so good (best when you are giving him a blowjob)

Examples of Dirty Talks After Sex

Post sex dirty talks are essential as it helps rebuild the excitement and anticipation of exploring each other's naked body again. As you bask in the euphoria of a hungry and intense sex session, you can further increase the sensuality using some of the dirty talks below.

284. Having your cum drip down my thighs is one of the best feelings I've ever had.

285. I could only wish we fuck all day forever.

286. Can't just help but think about how you fucked my brains out last night.

287. Did you study how to make me cum so quickly?

288. I feel like fucking you so hard in the shower.

289. I love holding your cock and feeling it get hard in my hands.

290. I had a naughty dream last night, and guess who's in it? The one I'm texting right now.

291. My body gets excited when you move your throbbing cock around my wet pussy.

292. You're the best baby. I was thinking about you last night before I went to sleep...

293. You've got the best cock I've ever seen.

294. I felt so good this morning when I remembered how good you fucked me last night.

295. What did you enjoy most about fucking me yesterday?

296. Having your cock inside me gives me orgasmic feelings.

297. Oh Yes! That was intense. Let's do it again even harder.

298. Having your cock inside me felt amazing. Fuck me again, baby.

299. You do know very well how to make me dripping wet with cum (this is a perfect message to boost his ego and make him want you more).

300. I love it when you wake me up with your tongue in my wet pussy.

301. I miss that feeling when your tongue lingers between my legs, right there at the top. I love how you cling to it with your tongue, oh! How it drives me crazy.

302. I love it when you slide my panties to one side, play with my pussy, then start to slowly slide your cock in... I can't stand it, but I want more.

303. Just the thought of you fucking me last night is making me wet.

304. I want you inside of me forever because I can't stop thinking about your cock every second.

305. Thinking about you is making me so horny, I can't stand it.

306. I want to suck your cock every second; I love how you taste.

307. I've got a new set of panties; I can't wait for you to see them on me.

308. Nobody has ever fucked me like you do.

309. I feel so weak and turned on at the same time when you hold me close.

310. You can't understand the feeling I get whenever I feel your cock in my pussy.

311. I love it when your sexy body is next to mine while I feel your parts.

312. I love it when I'm helpless and you are just diving your cock in me. Sexy!

313. I'm at your service tonight, do to me whatever you like.

314. Why can't I have you like this all the time? You are so hot.

315. Baby, tell me how badly you want me to fuck you right now.

316. Use me like your little fuck doll.

317. I can't help but wonder how you succeed in making me so damn wet within seconds.

318. I love it when you grab my hair and fuck me like you mean it.

319. You know what? I want to feel you so bad right now.

320. I'm wondering what is going on in that naughty mind... Are you ready for my next action?

321. Even when you're away, I can still feel your dick inside me. It's really hot.

322. Fuck me again and again! Let's lose the count of rounds. I want more!

323. I love feeling your dick in my hand, mouth, and pussy.

324. How much do you love it when you are riding and fucking me non-stop!

325. I love it when you make me cum with your tongue.

326. Making you hard is my number one priority.

327. I love it when you kiss me and lick me up.

328. Look how ready I am. Don't you want to put your dick in there?

329. I have never been fucked like this before. You feel so good!

330. Tell me all the dirty little things you do when you masturbate. Tell me everything, baby. Tell me how you play with yourself.

331. I think we have a problem; with the way you are always fucking me. I think I am so addicted to you.

332. Oh, baby, that was the best fuck I've ever had. You are the best. Thank you for that.

333. Touch yourself and let me watch you.

334. The rain made me wet today but having your hard cock inside me made me super wet.

335. Wow! That was orgasmic, baby. Let's do it again.

336. Oh, baby, I love it when you fuck me in both holes.

337. Kiss my pussy, and lick every inch of cum.

338. Do you want more of my wet pussy, come and get it!

339. I love the sound of your cock diving into my pussy all night long.

340. Baby, put your cock into my hole and fuck the hell out of me.

341. Come over here, baby, and dominate me like your little whore.

342. No breaks tonight, let's see how many times I can make you shoot your loads into me.

343. Do you like it when I spread my legs wide and take you in, baby?

344. Fill me up, baby, fuck my tight cunt! Make me scream with that big dick of yours.

345. I'm all yours tonight; you can have me anytime and anyhow you want.

346. Thinking about you gets me so wet that I can't wait to ride your cock hard.

347. Have you ever had the best blow job? Get ready for tonight; I will give you one.

348. I just had the most amazing reminisce of the steamy sex we had last night.

349. I love how big your dick/cock gets when you talk to me like this.

350. Oh baby, how I've missed your sexy muscular body. Come over here fuck my brains out.

351. I want you, baby. I want to make love to you. I want to enjoy sex with you. I want to fuck you.

352. Yes, baby, I feel so good when you make me cum like that.

353. Tell me what you want to do to me.

354. Rather than being at work, I imagine us naked together in bed right now.

355. Touch me right there; it feels so good.

356. I'm all yours tonight; you can wake me up any time you feel horny.

357. Baby, fill up that pussy. That's your pussy. Mark your fucking territory.

358. I'm supposed to be working, but all I'm thinking about is having another hot sex with you right now.

359. I'm going to slowly take your cock and tease it as it slides in and out of my pussy.

360. One day you will walk into the dining room, I'll be on the table and you can have me for dinner.

361. I'm going to massage you one night. I will oil you up, make you lay on your back, and then I will get naked

and rub my body all over your oily skin. Then I will slide my wet pussy onto you.

362. You will walk in one day and I will be laying on the table, covered in chocolate sauce and whipped cream. I will be your afternoon snack, and you will lick every bit of me clean.

363. If you could do anything to me tonight, what would you do?

364. Your face would look so great with me sitting on top of it.

365. I want to push you on the bed, take your clothes off and kiss you from your lips right down to the tip of your cock.

366. When I leave here and go home show me who owns this pussy.

367. That was amazing. I'm ready for round two when you are!

368. When I leave here and go home, Tell me how much you love it when you fuck my face.

369. Can we do this again tomorrow? I want to feel this way again

Chapter 13: Extra Tips to Help Your Shy Partner Open Up

Now, in your dirty talk dictionary, there are 369 dirty talks to build sexual tension, spice up the sexual experience, and boost after-sex pleasure. However, if your partner is a shy one, then you might have a problem with easing them into talking dirty. I know there is nothing more frustrating than having to teach someone the art

of talking dirty, and the person isn't getting it. Hence, this chapter covers some easy tips to enable your lover to overcome his shyness.

If you seek to open up your shy lover, you must first understand that it is a process that cannot be forced, neither can you rush it. It must be done effectively. Also, depending on the level of your partner's shyness, yours can be quick or slow.

Furthermore, you might not want to encourage him to say it on the first day. Imagine that you are in a 100 meters dash, and you want to win without starting at the start point but the endpoint; of course, you are going to be the first from last. Suppose you aim to assist your partner in surmounting his shyness. Here's a practical exercise for you.

Exercise one: encourage him to text it

An excellent way to quickly overcome shyness in your partner and open him up to talking dirty is to start using text, or better put, sext.

Bring up the idea of sex texting and encourage him to do it. Let's look at an example.

Jane: babe, I want you so bad.

Simon (the shy one): me too.

Jane: what do you want to do to me when you get back?

Simon: hmmm... I don't know.

Jane: c'mon. I know you can't wait to have me. Tell me.

Simon: why don't you wait and find out.

Jane: really? Don't you want me? I can't wait.

Simon: c'mon babe. You know I want you. (Jane's encouragement is starting to pay off)

Jane: what do you want to do to me? Can we make the sheets rough and sweaty?

Simon: I want to do many things to you. I can't wait to be home.

Jane: I know you want to do many things, but I want you to tell me. I'm horny.

Simon: I'm going to have sex with you like never before, and caress your body till you beg me to stop.

Jane: Oh, you are such a bad boy. I can't wait to do all that with you and lots more!

You don't need to say, *"talk dirty using text, baby."* You also don't need to bring it out and rush it right away with your partner. Be like Jane. Don't rush it, but push him out of his comfort zone. Encourage him, and he will give in to talking dirty. Mind you, don't expect him to talk dirty over and over again. Once he has given you a couple of dirty talks, you may consider letting it cool off and try another time unless you feel the mood still calls for a bit of talking dirty, and he is comfortable with it.

Exercise two: praise their improvement

Everyone loves praises and wouldn't mind hearing them every day of their life. So, learn to heap praises on your partner for talking dirty. You can start by using compliments like, *"oh, someone has been doing his homework." "Whoa, you are becoming my bad boy with those dirty talks."*

Also, you can introduce talking dirty using words at this stage. Give your compliment in words rather than texts and gauge his reaction. His reaction will determine if you should stick to texts for a while before going into word usage or if you should begin with words by using mild talks like, *"babe, are you free? I just got lingerie, and I want you to decide if it's sexy."*

Exercise three: tailor to what your partner likes

If you followed closely from the first chapter, I emphasized on the importance of understanding the words that are okay with your partner, and those that are a step-over-the-line. This is because they hold the key to success or failure in every dirty talk. If you want your partner to open up to talking dirty ideas, you need to tailor your words to his likes. Does he love a teddy bear? Talk teddy bear. Does he fancy your ass? Talk about it. Does he get turned on whenever you play with his nipples? Exploit it. Does he feel hyper whenever you mention a particular sex position? Talk about sex in that position.

I think you should understand what I mean. Use his likes only. I repeat **only!** No shy partner would want to talk about a body part they would have changed if they were to be God. So, leave out that body part that makes your lover feel horrible and use the likes that make him feel like a champ. This way, your partner won't be shy talking about it with you, and you would successfully open him up to talking dirty.

Exercise four: the kiss and whisper technique

This is a sensuous technique for opening up any shy lover. Indeed, you would kiss your lover a couple of times whenever you meet. Hence, whenever you kiss, trying whispering with your sexy voice. Say some spicy dirty talks and watch your partner giggle or respond to them.

When I use this technique, I usually whisper dirty talks like,

"Where else do you want to kiss me?"

"Oh, you kiss so passionately. I want more of you."

"You don't have an idea of how much I want you."

Whispering this after a kiss sends waves of pleasure and equally prompts a reply from the shy partner. Most times, the responses will surely be dirty talks, mostly if you have gone through exercises 1, 2, and 3.

Exercise five: compliment them

Finally, after you have encouraged him to text, introduced word usage, heaped praises on him, used the kiss, then whisper technique, then, it now comes down to your compliments.

Complimenting him for his efforts to become a dirty talker is a means to make him a dirty talker. It makes him want to do more, and in a short while, your partner cannot be shy when talking dirty to you. Dirty talking becomes normality.

Finally, talking dirty is an exciting idea that is useful in spicing up the sex life of couples. Shyness shouldn't be a barrier to benefiting from talking dirty. If you strictly follow these exercises, I bet you will easily surmount shyness and open-up your lover. However, if your partner isn't keen on talking dirty ideas, then it is best to look for something that works, a consensual sexual activity to spice up your sex life.

Conclusion

There's no such thing as the correct way to talk dirty. Dirty talk is subjective. Don't expect everything to go smoothly. Better yet, don't forget to laugh at any bloopers that you experience along the way. Remember that the key to a great relationship is when couples can laugh not at each other but with each other.

Practice makes perfect. This is true both in sex and in the art of dirty talking. The more you incorporate erotic phraseology in your sexy routine, the more you'll get better at it. That being said, the examples in this book are examples! Come up with your sexy lines. It's easy enough when the thought of your partner makes you think about the things you love most about him/her. Practice, seductive, mindful fucking. The next time you get it on, try to stay in the moment—relish the sensation and feeling in every session. Focus on the feeling, and the words will come to you. Do this with the utter confidence that no one in this world knows and understands your lover's body more than you do.

Don't feel compelled to say things you don't want to say so that you could please your partner. No matter how good of an actor/actress you are, your disgust will betray you. Keep in mind that you're exploring dirty talk not just for the pleasure of your lover but for your own too! So, sit down with your girlfriend/boyfriend or husband/wife and make up your own rules while taking into account each other's fantasies and limitations. Keep in mind that we base fantastic sex on mutual consideration for each other's desires.

Lastly, the greatest thing about talking dirty with your lover is that it opens up new doors for discovery. If you can talk like an expert seducer/seductress in bed, what other things can you do? Talking dirty is just the start of unraveling the deepest layers of your sexual persona. The confidence and the liberation that you gain from mastering the language of lust will set you towards the path to realizing your true carnal prowess, therefore allowing you to become the best lover that you can be.

References

https://www.mensjournal.com/health-fitness/the-complete-guide-to-dirty-talk-20150304/dont-worry-if-it-doesnt-work/

https://www.elitedaily.com/p/the-psychology-behind-dirty-talk-according-to-science-17298043

https://www.vixendaily.com/love/dirty-talk-phrases-guaranteed-to-make-him-turned-on/2/

https://www.medicaldaily.com/science-dirty-talk-and-why-it-increases-sexual-pleasure-349854

https://www.instyle.com/news/how-to-talk-dirty-even-if-you-are-shy

https://www.redonline.co.uk/health-self/relationships/a28113365/how-to-dirty-talk/

https://www.india.com/lifestyle/here-is-how-to-deal-with-sexual-inhibitions-and-have-the-much-deserved-pleasure-3941264/

https://www.bustle.com/p/how-to-overcome-sexual-hang-ups-with-your-partner-according-to-sex-therapists-56805